Praise for the work of Dr. Joseph Parent

"Doc does a great job teaching the all-important principles of the mental game for golf and everything you do."

—David Toms, PGA Champion and Ryder Cup player

"Dr. Parent has helped thousands of golfers to understand themselves and the game of golf better. Apply the ideas he recommends and I promise you will enjoy a deeper form of playing the game, which is what we are all striving for!"

—Dr. Fran Pirozzolo, PGA and LPGA Tours sports psychologist; mental skills coach for the New York Yankees and other world-class athletes

"We owe it all to *Zen Golf*!"

—Ray Romano and Kevin James, on winning the Celebrity Shoot-Out at the AT&T Pebble Beach National Pro-Am

"Zen Golf is an excellent book. I found many very valuable lessons that I am using to improve my game."

—Shigeki Maruyama, PGA Tour winner and #1 ranked golfer in Japan

"In the ever-growing body of golf wisdom books, this is a good one and well worth the read!"

—Michael Murphy, author of *Golf in the Kingdom*

"There is a lot more to being a great golfer than mechanics. Dr. Joe's writing and teaching go right to the heart of what you need to know to master the mental game."

—Dave LiCalsi, senior instructor for Dave Pelz Golf

"I love the insight and expertise that Dr. Parent brings to the game of golf. I've been reading his books for years, and they have helped me improve my golf game."

—Brittany Lincicome, LPGA Tour winner

"Working with Dr. Parent has helped me have greater awareness to synchronize body and mind for tournament golf."

—David Gossett, U.S. Amateur Champion and PGA Tour winner

"Soothing and enlightening, provocative and entertaining, *Zen Golf* exposes us to the storm-tossed waters of the golfer's psyche, but in short order Dr. Parent has us bobbing easily amidst the waves."

—Guy Yocom, senior writer for *Golf Digest*

"Dr. Parent taught me the mental game and helped me to get back in the winner's circle. *Zen Golf* is the way to be focused and get the most out of your game."

—Carlos Franco, PGA Tour Rookie of the Year 1999

"Deeply insightful but easy to understand, Dr. Parent's teaching helps golfers of all levels improve their golf game and their life as well."

—Michael Hunt, Lead Master Instructor, Jim McLean Golf Schools

"Dr. Parent's writing imparts the wisdom and techniques that will help you with your putting, your whole golf game, and your life as well."

—Deepak Chopra, M.D., author of *Golf for Enlightenment*

"*Zen Golf* is a really great book, with simple and clear lessons that can be applied to your game right away. *Zen Golf* gives you a new and better approach than other theories of sports psychology."

—Charles Howell III, PGA Tour Rookie of the Year 2001

"Dr. Joe gives golfers just what they need to keep their cool and play their best. I recommend his books to all my students."

—Katherine Roberts, fitness expert for the Golf Channel, ESPN Golf Schools, and author of *Yoga for Golfers*

"Doc's lessons really help. They are simple and fun, yet give you valuable knowledge that's very effective on the golf course."

—Len Mattiace, PGA Tour winner

ZEN

GOLF

doubleday

new york london toronto sydney auckland

ZEN
GOLF

mastering the mental game

Dr. Joseph Parent

PUBLISHED BY DOUBLEDAY
a division of Random House, Inc.
1540 Broadway, New York, New York 10036

DOUBLEDAY and the portrayal of an anchor with a dolphin are
trademarks of Doubleday, a division of Random House, Inc.

This book is not intended to take the place of medical advice from a
trained medical professional. Readers are advised to consult a
physician or other qualified health professional regarding treatment of
their medical problems. Neither the publisher nor the author take any
responsibility for any possible consequences from any treatment,
action, or application of medicine, herb, or preparation to any person
reading or following the information in this book.

Book design by Nicola Ferguson

Cataloging-in-Publication Data is on file
with the Library of Congress.

ISBN 0-385-50446-2

Copyright © 2002 by Joseph Parent

All Rights Reserved

PRINTED IN THE UNITED STATES OF AMERICA

June 2002

30 29 28 27 26 25 24 23

contents

CONTENTS

Part 2: The PAR Approach

CONTENTS

Part 3: A Game of Honor

acknowledgments

M any people helped make this book what it is. Foremost are my teachers, the Venerable Chögyam Trungpa, Rinpoche, and the Vajra Regent Ösel Tendzin (Thomas Rich, Jr.), as well as many other great masters of mind and meditation with whom I have had the privilege of studying. A special note of appreciation to Patrick Sweeney, the main student of Ösel Tendzin and my "brother" in Buddhist and Shambhala practice and study.

Ed Hanczaryk, a Shambhala golfer from the beginning, is a highly respected teaching professional now living in Nova Scotia. Our discussions about working with body, mind, and emotions in golf were the start of my coaching career. That was a long time and a lot of lessons ago. Thanks for everything, Ed.

Thanks as well to the rest of the charter members of the Shambhala Golfers Association, the band of gentle warriors that manifested the principles of Shambhala Golf with the inspiration and guidance of our teachers.

There can't be a teacher without students or a coach without players. To the many golfers who were willing to think outside the box and entrust their games to our work together, I am deeply grateful. Particular appreciation to touring professionals Brian Wilson, Willie Wood, Alex Quiroz, Shane Bertsch, Mike Meehan, Lisa Hackney, Rusty Clark, Jaxon Brigman, Landry Mahan, Mike Standly, John Rollins, Jeff Lowden, and Allan MacDonald.

To Jack and Barbara Nicklaus, much appreciation—to Jack for the inspiration of his unsurpassed mental game; to Barbara for her unsurpassed graciousness and kindness.

To Fred Shoemaker, gratitude for his friendship and for being the model of an ideal coach. To Dave LiCalsi of the Dave Pelz School, thanks for the conversations that went to the heart of the matter. To Michael Murphy, a toast to his inspiring vision of Golf in the Kingdom, set forth long before he ever heard about the kingdom of Shambhala.

To Casey Paulson and the staff at Rancho San Marcos Golf Course in Santa Barbara, thank you for welcoming me to coach at such a marvelous golf course and teaching/practice facility.

Thanks to Edward Sampson, Arlene Dorius, Jeff Herrick, Mimi Rich, Bruce Spears, Katherine Butterfield, Randy Sunday, Irv and Leah Mermelstein, Glen Kakol, Sandy Saunderson, and David Yossem for their part in expanding the vision and path of this adventure. Thanks to the many other dear friends of the Ojai Valley Dharma Center and other meditation centers who supported and encouraged my work in teaching golf as a vehicle for practicing awareness and manifesting Shambhala warriorship.

Many thanks to my editor, Jason Kaufman of Doubleday, for his vision, insights, and guidance. Great appreciation to my literary agent, Angela Rinaldi. She is also a gifted editor who nurtured this book from seed to blossoming flower. Angela, you're the best.

Thanks to the friends who reviewed and commented on the manuscript, especially Steve Moore, my assistant coach/golf school coordinator, and fellow author and golf partner Ken Zeiger, for their enthusiastic involvement and insightful suggestions.

Last but not least, deep gratitude to my whole family for their encouragement in my work on this book. A special salute to Mom for her generous and enthusiastic support. My sister Nancy, a brilliantly creative writer and editor, provided invaluable help in every step of this book's evolution. Nan, you have no idea what a joy it has been to work with you.

To the Venerable Chögyam Trungpa, Rinpoche, who brought the teachings of Shambhala warriorship to the West and showed me the true nature of mind.

And to his heart son and lineage holder, Vajra Regent Ösel Tendzin, who taught me how to manifest the vision of Shambhala warriorship in golf and in life.

introduction

I'm a golf coach, but I don't instruct golfers on their swings. I teach them how to use their minds on the golf course and how to play from their hearts. I try to give golfers a different way of thinking about how they play the game and how they treat themselves on the golf course. I teach golfers how to play "Zen golf."

Zen means "action with awareness," being completely in the present moment. The qualities that accompany the Zen experience include expansive vision, effortless focus, a feeling of equanimity and timelessness, abundant confidence, and complete freedom from anxiety or doubt. Interestingly, this is exactly the way champion athletes describe "being in the Zone." It is also strikingly similar to the way golfers describe the feeling of a perfectly struck golf shot, a feeling every golfer wants to have again and again.

Harvey Penick, the revered golf teacher, said, "All seasoned players know, or at least have felt, that when you are playing your best, you are much the same as in a state of meditation. You're free of tension and chatter. You are concentrating on one thing. It is the ideal condition for good golf."

In the last twenty years, golf equipment such as clubs, balls, and training aids, including the use of video for swing analysis, have improved tremendously. Swing instruction books and magazines are more plentiful now than ever. Still, no appreciable improvement in the average golfer's scores has resulted. Why?

No matter how sophisticated their equipment or their knowledge about the swing, if golfers don't know how to work with their minds on the course, they encounter the common mental obstacles that keep them from realizing their potential. Performance anxiety, emotional reactions, and distractions interfere with golfers' abilities. Overcoming such obstacles is the key to breaking through to lower scores. The stories and lessons in *Zen Golf: Mastering the Mental Game* are about freeing ourselves from fear and doubt, and activating confidence—what every golfer needs.

The principles of *Zen Golf* evolved from my study and practice of Buddhist meditation and psychology, as well as an enduring passion for golf. One of my meditation teachers, Ösel Tendzin, was an avid golfer. He used golf outings as a setting for communication with his students. After a round of golf, he would talk with us about the connection between golf, meditation, and the teachings of Shambhala warriorship, a companion tradition to Buddhism. Shambhala warriorship emphasizes fearlessness and dignity and is similar to the mind-set of martial arts traditions like Zen archery. These experiences with my teacher gave me a different perspective on the game, one that formed the basis for my coaching and the lessons in *Zen Golf.*

Tiger Woods, in an ABC-TV interview, said, "My mother's a Buddhist. In Buddhism, if you want to achieve enlightenment, you have to do it through meditation and self-improvement through the mind. That's something she's passed on to me: to be able to calm myself down and use my mind as my main asset."

Many books and articles on the mental game will tell you, "Stay in the present, keep focused, clear your mind, don't get down on yourself." What makes *Zen Golf* special is that it teaches you *how* to do those things, with time-tested mindfulness and awareness techniques and exercises for working with thoughts and emotions, for settling and centering your body and mind, for changing unhelpful habits.

In the Buddhist tradition there is a saying that for an activity to be fruitful, it must be good in the beginning, good in the middle, and good at the end. Through years of playing, practicing, and coaching the mental game of golf, three aspects emerged as the ideal beginning, middle, and end for any golf shot. I refer to them as the *PAR Approach* to golf instruction—*p*reparation, *a*ction, and *r*esponse to results. This is the organizing principle of my coaching program for golf schools and corporate outings, for teaching every level of golfer from PGA professional to beginning amateur.

As you'll read in this book, the keys to *preparation* are clarity, commitment, and composure. These are necessary for developing a sound, consistent routine. The ideal state of mind for *action* is feeling confident, focused, and in the flow, with body and mind synchronized in the present moment. This allows you to execute a shot free from the interference of mental chatter or paralysis from analysis. The best *response to results* is one that enhances future performance. You'll be introduced to a unique "post-shot routine." This special way of relating to the outcome of a shot is highly effective in fostering confidence by building on success and learning from mistakes without negativity.

Continued success at golf (and any other endeavor) requires all three aspects: preparation, action, and response to results. They form the framework for the instructions presented in *Zen Golf*. Applied properly, they will help you achieve focus, calmness, and confidence, the most essential ingredients of peak performance.

Zen Golf will also introduce you to a unique perspective that brings together techniques of modern psychology, experiences of generations of golfers, and the ancient wisdom of the Buddhist and Shambhala traditions. Rather than an instruction manual that takes you through a systematic program like a cookbook, it is a collection of brief chapters offering the wisdom of traditional Zen stories and teachings applied in actual lessons with golfers, many of whom are PGA professionals.

The opening section of *Zen Golf*, "A Different Perspective," introduces a new way of thinking about your game. Instead of always asking, "What's wrong with me?" you can learn to focus on what's *right* with you.

The instructional section of *Zen Golf* teaches the stages of the PAR Approach. Many of the chapters in this section focus on putting and the short game, because the hopes and fears that create mental obstacles intensify as we get closer to our objective: the ball going into the hole. You'll be given instruction in mindfulness and awareness practice, the cornerstones of mastering the mental game. In particular, you'll learn a powerful technique that transforms habits quickly, with a minimum of effort.

The concluding section of *Zen Golf,* "A Game of Honor," looks at the ways in which the game of golf offers opportunities to manifest the hallmarks of warriorship: dignity, confidence, and genuineness.

In *Zen Golf* you'll learn ways to make your mind an ally instead of an enemy, how to stay calm, avoid mental mistakes, reduce frustration, increase consistency, and lower your scores.

Many of my students feel that the methods of *Zen Golf* benefit them in other areas of their lives. It is my hope that this book will help you tap into the unconditional confidence that is already there in your heart. May it enable you to ride the ups and downs you encounter with poise, humor, and humility, making the game of golf and the game of life ever more rewarding for yourself and your playing companions.

PART 1

A Different Perspective

Confidence is an unconditional state in which you simply possess an unwavering state of mind that needs no reference point. There is no room for doubt; even the question of doubt does not occur. . . . This unconditional confidence contains gentleness, because the notion of fear does not arise; sturdiness, because in the state of confidence there is ever-present resourcefulness; and joy, because trusting in the heart brings a greater sense of humor. This confidence can manifest as majesty, elegance, and richness in a person's life.

—Venerable Chögyam Trungpa,
*Shambhala: The Sacred Path
of the Warrior*

empty your cup

A young man had read all the books he could find about Zen. He heard about a great Zen master and requested an appointment with him to ask for teachings. When they were seated, the young man proceeded to tell the master everything he had understood from his reading, saying that Zen is about this and Zen is about that, on and on.

After some time, the master suggested that they have tea. He performed the traditional tea ceremony while the student sat at attention, bowing when served, saying nothing. The master began to pour tea into the student's cup. He poured until it was full, and kept pouring. The tea ran over the edge of the cup and onto the table. The master kept pouring as the tea ran off the table and onto the floor. Finally, the student couldn't contain himself any longer. He shouted, "Stop! Stop pouring! The cup is full—no more will go in!"

The master stopped pouring and said, "Just like this cup, your mind is full of your own opinions and preconceptions. How can you learn anything unless you first empty your cup?"

Many golfers have read volumes about the golf swing. They come to a lesson with so many ideas about their swing that they can't hear anything that the pro has to say. They come to the lesson with a full cup.

The empty cup approach doesn't mean giving up your intelligence and following blindly. The point is to receive everything that's taught in an open way, withholding judgment about it until you've tried it for a while. Try your best to understand what is being communicated, then give it a fair chance to see whether or not it works for you.

Shunryu Suzuki Roshi, a great Zen master, said, "In the beginner's mind there are many possibilities; in the expert's mind there are few." Beginner's mind is a mind that is open, eager to learn, an empty cup. If your mind is open, empty of preconceptions, it is always inquisitive, receptive to whatever arises, and ready to engage.

Whether we practice meditation or golf or anything else, at first our experience is fresh and illuminating. When we begin, we have no thoughts of having already accomplished something. Then we can learn. But after a while, it can get stale. We may think we know something and lose our motivation. Our cup starts to fill, and there is less room for something new. When we become aware that this is happening, we can take a fresh start and return to beginner's mind. We may find it challenging to keep to our beginner's mind. But it is so worthwhile. With beginner's mind we can learn from everyone and everything we encounter.

Ben Hogan was perhaps the best ball-striker of all time,

with the most precise swing ever. Yet he never tired of practice. In fact, he delighted in it. That's because he believed there was always more to learn. He always had beginner's mind.

four kinds of students

There's a saying, "Golf can't be taught, it can only be learned." That doesn't mean we can do without instruction. The point is that no matter how good the instruction is, it is only as useful as the student's interest and effort in learning. In describing the learning process, the Buddhist teachings once again make use of the metaphor of the cup. Four types of cups symbolize four kinds of students. Instruction is symbolized by water being poured.

The first cup is upside down. This represents a student who is supposedly there to learn, but pays no attention. You may have experienced something similar while reading a book: Your eyes move across the words all the way down the page, but when you get to the bottom, you realize you were daydreaming and have no idea what you read. That's what happens when a cup is turned upside down. No matter how much is poured, nothing gets in.

The second cup is right side up, but has a hole in the bottom. We hear what's being taught, but we forget it all too soon.

We don't chew on it and digest it and take it to heart. For example, we might attend a golf school, and when we get home, be asked by a friend, "What did they teach?" And we say, "Um, well, it was . . . Actually, I don't remember." This is the classic case of "in one ear and out the other."

The third cup is right side up and doesn't have a hole in it, but the inside is covered with dirt. When the clear water of instruction is poured in, the dirt makes it cloudy. This symbolizes the way we can distort what we hear, interpreting and editing it to fit into our preconceived ideas or opinions. Nothing new is actually learned. When we take a lesson, if the instruction matches how we already see things, it is taken as confirmation. Anything new that doesn't match our opinion is resisted, ignored, or disregarded.

The fourth cup represents the ideal way to be a student. It is upright, receiving what is taught. It has no holes, retaining what is taught. It is clean, open to learning something new. To whatever extent you can, be like the fourth cup.

Most golfers profess to want to improve their games. When people find out that I coach the mental game, many of them say, "Boy, do I need that." But most aren't really interested in learning—like upside-down cups.

Sometimes at the end of a golf school session, before we play the course or practice, I emphasize a particular thing to do in connection with every shot. Later when I ask how it went, half the group had forgotten to do it at all. Right through the bottom of the cup.

When people come back for a second lesson, I ask about

the practice I gave them to do at home. The descriptions are sometimes so different from what was said that I barely recognize them. Those cups already had a whole lot in them that got mixed up with what was taught.

But it's delightful when someone who, like the fourth type of cup, comes back and describes the results of working on what we discussed, and has even begun to apply the instruction to other aspects of his or her game.

The most gratifying experience of all is when a student says, "Wait a minute, Doc. This has to do with a lot more than golf, doesn't it?"

thinking outside
the box

My golf schools often start with a little puzzle called the Nine Dots Exercise.

Connect these nine dots with only four straight lines without lifting your pencil from the paper. You may cross a line you've already drawn. (The solution is on the next page.)

    •   •   •

    •   •   •

    •   •   •

To complete the Nine Dots Exercise, you need to go outside the artificial limits of the "box" that the nine dots seem to define. If you assume you have to stay within the box, four continuous straight lines will always leave at least one dot unconnected.

Here's the solution: Start at the upper left dot and (1) draw a horizontal line through the top row and go *past* the upper right dot about an inch. Then (2) from that point draw a diagonal line through the right dot of the middle row and middle dot of the bottom row, *past* it about an inch to a point directly below the left dot of the bottom row. Then (3) from that point draw a vertical line up through the bottom and middle left dots to the top left dot. Then (4) from the top left dot draw a diagonal line through the middle dot of the middle row and the right dot of the bottom row. You've connected all nine dots with only four straight lines, without lifting your pencil from the paper.

Thus, to solve the puzzle, your lines have to go beyond the right edge of the imagined box and then beyond the bottom of the imagined box. In other words, you have to *think outside the box.*

The point of this exercise is to show how we limit ourselves by our assumptions. Looking at things with a big mind, with a larger or different perspective, increases our choices dramatically. It allows for so much more creativity.

Once Tiger Woods was watching a friend of his who was paired with one of my players in a Qualifying School tournament. We were discussing how the players were planning to approach a particular par-5 hole. The green was tucked in behind some trees on the right, and most players who tried to hit the green in two shots ended up in those trees. The only other option seemed to be laying up with their second shot in the fairway about ninety yards short of the green and hitting a sand wedge from there. Tiger said that he would do it differently. He'd play a long second shot, but aim at the rough to the left of the green. It wasn't very deep, and from there it was an easy short pitch onto the green and a very good chance for a tap-in birdie.

Most golfers play inside the box made by the edges of the fairways and the greens. Few would intentionally aim for the rough. Seeing the possibility of taking such an unconventional approach exemplifies the ability to "think outside the box."

par for the course

"Par" is an example of an illusory "box" that mid- to high-handicap golfers create for themselves. They would do well to think outside of it.

Less than 1 percent of all golfers have completed a round of golf in par or better. That makes it a rather unrealistic target score for all but the most skilled among us. Measuring yourself against the par on the scorecard is a setup for failure for the average golfer.

Another problem with par is that it is printed on score-cards and signs. When it was first used, the number set as "par for the course" varied according to the difficulty of the course conditions under which a competition was played. If it was played in a howling wind and driving rain on a long, tight golf course, par might have been set at 85 that day. A scorecard doesn't change with the weather. Would you expect to shoot the same score at your home course on a cold, rainy, windy day as on a sunny and calm day? Unlikely. How about when they've narrowed the fairways and let the rough grow for a tournament? No, again. So why measure your score against the same number in widely different conditions?

I suggest that you set your own par for the course. Change the par written on the scorecard to reflect your handicap, as well as the conditions, making it your "personal par for the day." Before each round, on your scorecard, cross out and rewrite the par given to each of the harder holes on the course. Add one for as many holes as you receive handicap strokes (and one or two more if the weather or course conditions are extra challenging). The harder par-4 holes are now par-5s, etc.

For high handicappers (over 18), on some holes your "personal par" will be two strokes higher than the par on the scorecard. You will become much more at ease approaching a difficult hole from this new perspective. It will also encourage more patience in recovering from a mis-hit, knowing you have that extra stroke or two to get to the green.

You'll also feel much better at the end of a hole or the end of a round by using this perspective-changing technique. For a 20-handicapper playing the hardest hole, instead of dejectedly saying, "I made another double-bogey," you get to say, "I made my par!" at the end of your round, instead of saying, "I shot a ninety-one," you get to say, "I finished at one under par!" It's pretty clear which will make you feel more encouraged about this round and more confident about the next one.

Some might say this could lead to complacency. However, I've found it will actually enhance your interest in improving your game and lowering your handicap. In this way, you can gradually reduce your personal par. The idea of reaching the par on the scorecard seems an insurmountable task when it is twenty strokes away. Getting there little by little with rewards along the way is much more workable.

cover the roads with leather

Somewhere in ancient India, there was a king whose feet were very sensitive. He complained constantly about the kingdom's roads, which were rough and rocky. Finally, the king decided he would have all the roads covered with leather, so that he could walk on leather anywhere he wanted to go and his feet would be comfortable.

He invited the best craftsmen in the land to bid on this formidable project. One replied, "I can do the job, but it will cost all that is in the kingdom's treasury." Another said, "I can cover the roads with leather for half of what is in the treasury." Then an old woman came to the king and said, "I can do the job for ten rupees. I'll just strap a piece of leather under each of your feet, and you'll be walking on leather wherever you go."

When things aren't the way we'd like them to be, there's a tendency to complain. This is certainly true for golfers. "It's windy." "It's cold." "The greens are too bumpy." "The rough is too deep." "The fairways are too narrow." "There aren't enough parking spaces." And on and on.

Jack Nicklaus said that at many tournaments he felt he only had to beat a few of his fellow competitors. When he'd hear players complain about conditions, he'd check them off one by one, thinking to himself, "There's a guy who won't be in contention." "There's another one I don't have to worry about." By the time the tournament started, not many were left.

Complaining, wanting all the conditions to be just the way we'd like them, doesn't get us anywhere. In fact, we're just distracting ourselves from the task at hand. Instead of complaining, recognize that everyone has to play the same course. Sure, there are times when the morning groups have bad weather and it clears for the player teeing off in the afternoon, or vice versa. So what? Golf and life aren't fair on a day-to-day basis. But those good and bad breaks even out over the long run.

Learn to play a variety of conditions. Adapt yourself and your state of mind to whatever you encounter. Cover your feet with leather, and you'll be walking comfortably no matter how rough the road.

My teacher Ösel Tendzin gave one of his students this very powerful instruction about complaining. It has three parts:

> Don't complain
> About anything
> Not even to yourself.

how big is your mind?

How big is your mind? Is it the same size as your brain? Does it have a shape? Is it located in a particular spot?

A Zen master asked a student, "Where is your mind?"

The student said, "When I perceive my thoughts, it is as if someone were speaking inside my head. So my mind must be in my head."

The master motioned for the student to approach him. When the student stood right in front of him, the master banged his fist down on the student's big toe and said, "Now where is your mind?"

If we notice a sensation in our foot, it is actually experienced in our mind. So perhaps our mind is the size of our body. But we also experience what we see, so perhaps our mind is as big as our field of vision. What if I asked you to imagine the farthest star in the farthest galaxy? Now how big is your mind?

Ultimately, our mind has the potential to be as big as the universe. The more open our mind, the bigger it is. The more consumed by worry and petty concerns, the smaller it is. Tunnel vision might be very focused, but if you miss a critical variable in your planning, the shot will be a disaster. Temper tantrums make for a very small mind and lead to awful decisions. Worrying about missing a four-foot putt makes your mind feel about as tiny as a thimble. Playing your best golf comes from having the biggest mind. Whatever you encounter, connect with the space around it, see it in as big a context as you can. Look at the lay of the land and start reading your putt when you're fifty yards from the green. See the big view.

If we get "ball-bound" before we swing, we lose track of the space we're sending the ball into. A small mind interferes with making a free swing that follows through toward the target. After a good drive or iron shot, watch it fly, without a lot of comment, just appreciating the whole picture. Notice how open and expansive, how big, your mind feels. Connect with that experience and call it up before your next shot. You'll be surprised how much more you see and feel.

Big Mind Exercise

On a level area of the putting green, place a ball about twenty feet from a hole, with the flag removed. Set up for the putt, focusing on the hole, and get a feel for the distance from the ball to the hole. Instead of stroking the putt, stand up and turn to face the hole. Now close your eyes, walk toward the hole, and, holding the putter by the head, try to put the grip end of the putter into the hole. (Don't count your steps; just put the putter grip down when you think you've gotten to the hole.)

How did you do? Most people stop short of the hole. They may start taking smaller, tentative steps as they get near the point where they think the hole is, as if they're not allowed to go past it. The hole is the assumed limit, the end of the "box" they can't go outside of. Their mind is only as big as the space between the ball and the hole.

Now set up to the putt again, but this time look beyond the hole. Expand your view to the far edge of the green, then come back to the hole, seeing it within the larger space. Now walk again with eyes closed and try to put the grip end of the putter in the hole. This time you were probably much closer to the hole, or even a little bit beyond it. That's the impact of letting your mind be bigger.

When you focus tightly on the hole, your mind is smaller and your world is more constricted. The first time you did the exercise, you probably slowed down as you thought you were getting near the hole. If the hole were at "the edge of the world," you would be careful not to go beyond it and fall off.

If we focus so tightly on the hole that there's nothing in our mind past it, it becomes the edge of *our* world. We don't want to send our ball over the edge, so we subconsciously try to just barely get it to the hole.

There is also an optical counterpart to this psychological effect. Visually focusing tightly on an object foreshortens the perceived distance to that object. In other words, it looks closer than it actually is. Combine that with being afraid to go past the hole, and the ball never gets there. That's one reason why we leave our putts short so often.

When getting ready to putt, let your view include more of the green and see the distance to the hole within that bigger space.

Bigger space, bigger mind. Bigger mind, better results.

you are not
your thoughts

The student respectfully approached the master, bowed, and requested instruction.

"My mind is very difficult to control," he explained. "When I want some thoughts to go, they stay. When I want others to stay, they go. How can I control my mind?"

The master said, "The mind is like a high-spirited wild horse. If you try to control it by locking it up, it will be agitated and restless. If you try to force it to be still, it will kick and fight even more.

"Take a bigger view of control. Within the big meadow of awareness, let the wild horse of your mind run here and there. With nothing to struggle against, it will eventually settle down on its own. When it has settled, you can tame it; when it is tame, you can train it. Then you can ride the horse of your mind, and it will swiftly take you wherever you want to go."

Many times I've heard golfers lament, "I know I have the talent, if only I could get out of my own way." What is it that's in the way? Most of the time, it's your thoughts.

While playing well in a tournament, we might think to ourselves, "Well, you've gotten away with it so far, but you'll screw up before too long." Believing in this thought gives it power. It creates feelings of doubt and anxiety, which interfere with our swing and produce errant shots. That makes us believe the thought even more, amplifying it in our mind. Eventually, the fear of failure becomes so powerful that our game is badly disrupted and the prophecy of the thought has been fulfilled.

Yet aren't thoughts our own creations? Why would we knowingly create something that interferes with what we intend to accomplish? Let's take a closer look at our thoughts—and how we relate to them—from a different perspective.

Usually, it feels as if our thoughts and our mind are one

and the same. Our thoughts seem to completely fill our mind. It's as if we are in a continuous stream of conversation with ourselves. Without hesitation we act on these thoughts and fears instead of having the freedom to choose whether or not to respond.

Does it have to be this way? If we look carefully, we can see that thoughts arise *in* our mind, but they are *not* our mind. By observing our thoughts and the feelings that precede and follow them, we can begin to experience a gap in the sequence of impulse-to-thought-to-action, and we can choose how to *respond* rather than automatically *react*.

Awareness of Thoughts

The practice of working with thoughts is fundamental to Buddhism. To begin, sit upright on a chair or cross-legged on a cushion, remaining as quiet as possible. Eyes open, gaze slightly lowered, rest your attention lightly on the breath. This has a settling effect on body and mind. Let your awareness include bodily sensations and other perceptions, without letting them distract you from the breath.

As thoughts arise, you simply let them come up and go by, neither inviting them to stay nor trying to get rid of them. Noticing them is enough; there's no need for analyzing or judging them.

Doing this for just a little while creates the space that allows you to gain insight into the quality of thoughts. They come and go in your mind, but they don't have to occupy it completely.

Doing this awareness practice regularly begins to change your relationship to your thoughts. You begin to see the contrast between being off somewhere in the past or future and being here in the present. When you're present, you are simply being aware. Whatever thoughts or feelings come up, you can be aware of them without having to act on them.

There may be moments when little or no mental chatter occupies your mind. In that space of simply being, whatever sights, sounds, smells, or sensations you experience become vivid and clear.

In Buddhism, mind and awareness are synonymous. Awareness is open and spacious, the container of whatever is experienced. Like a mirror, it does not have any particular color or content of its own, but reflects whatever appears. Thoughts, sense perceptions, emotional feelings, and dreams all appear in your mirrorlike mind. None of these *are* the mind; they all arise as *contents* of the mind. You have thoughts, but you are not your thoughts.

When you identify with awareness instead of its contents, small mind becomes big mind. You can see each thought as a little cloud floating across the big sky of your mind.

With this perspective, you can recognize the nature of thoughts as words and pictures passing through your mind, with no more tangible reality than images on a movie screen. Revealed for what they are, thoughts lose their power. Watching them come and go, dissolving as easily as they arose, you have a choice about what you pay attention to and what you disregard. They have power only to the extent that you give it to them.

In golf it is extremely valuable to be able to relate to your thoughts without being compelled by them. Late in a match, the thought might arise to go for the green on a long shot over a pond when the risk far outweighs the reward. At moments like that, you need to take a step back, get things in perspective, and not make emotional decisions that could cost you the chance to win a match or tournament. Think of how many strokes you would save every round if there were a little bit of space and time between your thoughts arising and your acting on them.

basic goodness

A young man had a clay statue, a family heirloom. He'd always wished that it were bright shiny gold instead of plain brown clay. When he began to earn a living, he put aside a little now and then, until he had enough for his special project: to have his statue covered with gold.

Now it looked just the way he wanted it to, and people admired it. He felt very proud that he had a gold statue. However, the gold-plating didn't stick to the clay very well, and it wasn't long before it began to flake off in spots. So he had it gold-plated again. Soon he found himself using all his time and resources to maintain the gold facade of his statue.

One day his grandfather returned from a journey of many years. The young man wanted to show him how he had made the clay statue into a gold one. However, clay was showing through in many spots, so he was somewhat embarrassed.

The old man smiled and held the statue lovingly. With a moist cloth he gently rubbed it and gradually dissolved some of the clay. "Many years ago, the statue must have fallen in the mud and become covered with it. As a very young child, you wouldn't have known the difference. You forgot, and thought it was just a clay statue. But look here."

He showed his grandson the place where the clay was removed, and a bright yellow color shone through. "Underneath the covering of clay, your statue has been solid gold from the very beginning. You never needed to put more gold on to cover the clay. Now that you know what its nature really is, all you have to do is gently remove the clay and you'll reveal the gold statue you've possessed all along."

One of the most fundamental principles of the Buddhist and Shambhala traditions, as taught by my teacher Chögyam Trungpa, is that the true nature of human beings is basic goodness. As he said, "This is not a matter of talking yourself into believing that everything is okay; you are genuine and good just as you are." It is the simple, direct appreciation of being alive that is common to everyone. Golfers recognize it in that moment after a seemingly effortless swing sends a golf ball soaring into the sky.

It is a perspective of richness, wholeness, that nothing in our fundamental being is flawed or missing. Acknowledging our own basic goodness means taking the attitude that there is something fundamentally, essentially right with us. How we feel about ourselves as a person doesn't need to depend on the quality of a particular golf shot or the outcome of a round.

That perspective is very different from the attitude most prevalent in the world today. There is a need to prove our worth again and again, that stems from the underlying view that there is something fundamentally wrong with us. We think that in order to be who we *want* to be, we need to be something different than what we are. This is "poverty mentality," the feeling that we're not good enough, that we're broken and need to be fixed, that we're missing something that needs to be added to make us whole. Like the gold statue, over the years our basic goodness has become covered over by self-doubt and fear. Our memory of your natural contentment has faded, and we think that the way out of our feelings of inadequacy is to gold-plate ourselves into looking better.

We usually relate to our golf game from that kind of poverty mentality. It's all too common on the course to hear self-deprecating remarks summed up in that plaintive cry after a dismal shot: "What's wrong with me?" Sometimes it seems as if we live or die according to how well or poorly we execute a golf shot.

Our swing is the gold statue of our golf game. When we make a poor shot, we usually assume that something is wrong with our swing. Therefore, we think we need to do something to fix it, to add something to it to make it whole, to change something about it to make it right. That's like adding gold plate on top of clay.

Quick fixes and patch-up jobs during a round will only take you further and further from understanding what you're doing when you swing, just as adding more gold on top of the clay takes us further from the real gold underneath. However, by not fixing your swing you will start to recognize patterns and be more realistic in your targets and yardages. Seeing the patterns in your shots without trying to change them will allow you to be more aware of what you're doing to produce them. That gives you the information and insight you need to go to the practice tee (or lesson tee) and work on changing your habits.

We don't need to gold-plate our swing; we just need to dissolve the clay of interference that obscures the pure gold of what our body already knows how to do. Taking this different perspective means transforming our poverty mentality into a "richness mentality." Recognizing basic goodness as our own nature becomes the impetus for discovering unconditional confidence.

Then the wayward shots no longer become punishment or confirmation of our failings, but clues that help us discover how to remove more and more clay so that our game can eventually shine like solid gold.

unconditional confidence

How well we play golf is often a reflection of our level of confidence. We'd all like to have the feeling that every drive will find the fairway and every putt will find the hole.

It's important to recognize that there are three kinds of confidence.

False confidence. False confidence doesn't help at all. It's just talking big, kidding ourselves. It can lead to taking unrealistic chances, usually with disastrous consequences. We may be trying to impress others into thinking we're better than we actually are. The truth comes out in no time on the golf course.

Conditional confidence. This kind of confidence depends on recent results. We are confident "on the condition" that we continue to play well. When things go well, our confidence can build until we feel like we can make every shot. But if things go badly, we start questioning our ability. We start asking, "What's wrong with me?" From there, down we go. If we're worried that we might hit a bad shot and we do, we feel even less confident for the next one. It's a self-fulfilling prophecy. The antidote to this is unconditional confidence.

Unconditional confidence. Unconditional confidence arises from connecting with our basic goodness. We believe in ourselves as decent people and in our golfing skills for our level of play. This doesn't mean that we expect to hit every shot perfectly. It does mean that we can handle whatever the result is. With unconditional confidence, our self-worth as a human being doesn't depend on how well or poorly we strike a golf ball. We see our nature and our abilities as basically good and the difficulties we encounter as temporary experiences. Instead of assuming something is wrong with our swing and trying to fix it, we reflect on what may have interfered with our intention on that shot. This approach makes it possible to quickly turn things around and play well again.

Unconditional confidence takes a big perspective, independent of moment-to-moment results. The bigger the perspective we have, the better we can ride the inevitable ups and downs within a round, over several rounds, or even longer. We can handle difficulties with a sense of humor, knowing that these things come and go. We can regard experiences of success with a sense of humility; these also come and go. Whatever we encounter, we can be fearless in the moment. That's the expression of true confidence.

clearing the interference

According to the dictionary, to enlighten means to shed the light of truth and knowledge upon; to free from ignorance and error. An enlightened approach to golf means seeing things from a different perspective. It means swinging freely, playing the game in a way that is free from interference.

Rather than labor under the clouds of fear, doubt, and frustration, we can clear them from our mind and tap into our inherent confidence. Like the sun appearing from behind the clouds, if we clear away the interference, our confidence will come shining through.

Clearing away interference involves two steps. First, it requires *recognition*. For example, we might have a habit of sabotaging every good round that we play, messing up the last few holes. If we don't realize what's going on, we might think there are problems with our swing and try any number of "fixes" that don't address the real issue. We need to cultivate awareness of what is actually getting in the way of playing our best.

The second step is *undoing*. Again, the point is not so much that something is missing. Rather, something is in the way. It's less about learning something new than unlearning something old. An ostrich doesn't have to get a new head; it just has to lift the one it already has out of the sand. If we are sabotaging ourselves and we recognize that, we can begin to change our habits. Once we remove the self-defeating behavior, nothing will be in the way of playing our best.

a perfect swing

I'd like to congratulate you. You have a perfect swing. Now, you're probably thinking, "What's that about? He's never seen my swing." Well, I don't need to, because I didn't say *the* perfect swing (which, by the way, doesn't exist, since we are all as different as snowflakes). I said *a* perfect swing, and everyone has one. Your perfect swing is the best one you can make today. It can be improved later through more learning and practice, but right now it's the best one you've got. It's the one you brought with you, and it's the only one to dance with.

The question is, do we make that perfect swing every time? Certainly not. Although you can't make a better swing than the one you brought today (we get into trouble when we try to), you can definitely interfere with it and make it worse. Too often we judge our swing, ready to criticize our shots, feeling self-conscious and uptight. That's why I like to say, "Looking over your own shoulder can give you a real pain in the neck."

You don't forget how to swing from one shot to the next. It's just that things get in the way. We often get a poor result, analyze our swing, and try to fix it, only to have our "fix" interfere with the next swing. Then we try to "fix" that swing, and soon we have so many fixes that our mind feels like a pretzel and we have no idea how to swing the strange-feeling instrument in our hands. It's usually around the sixteenth or seventeenth hole that we give up and just swing. Amazingly, our swing is back. We might think that it had been lost and at last we found it, but in fact we never lost it. Like the gold statue described earlier, our swing was just covered in the clay of interference. When we gave up fixing our swing, the absence of interference allowed it to reappear.

If you make a swing that falls short of perfect (for you), don't get down on yourself or try to fix your swing. Instead, direct your awareness to reflect on what might have interfered. Most interference originates in the way we prepare for a shot. The basic point is: Don't change your swing, change your mind. Clear the interference, then trust your own perfect swing, and it will give you the most consistent results. This is the fundamental perspective of *Zen Golf*.

PART 2

The PAR Approach:

PREPARATION

ACTION

RESPONSE TO RESULTS

Ask yourself how many shots you would have saved if you always developed a strategy before you hit, always played within your capabilities, never lost your temper, and never got down on yourself.

—Jack Nicklaus

PREPARATION

Preparation is the first stage of the PAR Approach. The key factors in preparation are the three Cs: clarity, commitment, and composure. *Clarity* is having a vivid image of the shot you intend, both the target and the path the ball will take to get there. *Commitment* is being free from second-guessing, doubt, or hesitation. *Composure* is being calm and focused, poised and at ease. These are what you need to be properly prepared to play a shot. The material in this section progresses through these concepts, helping you make the three Cs part of your game. When you do, they'll add up to the most important C of all *Confidence.*

what is your target?

Our actions are shaped by our intentions. When I ask golfers the purpose of making a golf swing, most of them answer, "To hit the ball." Yet focusing on the ball as the target is a problematic perspective. Thinking of their job as "hitting the ball" instead of "sending the ball to a target" is probably why you see some high handicappers make quite acceptable practice swings and then get up to the ball and swing like they're chopping wood. When the purpose of the swing is to send the ball to a target, that's a different intention and a different swing appears. Set up to a shot with those two different intentions (hitting the ball versus sending it into the distance) and notice the difference in your stance and mental focus. "Sending it" calls forth a stance and state of mind that are far better preparation for a successful golf shot.

Even accomplished golfers sometimes fall victim to an unhelpful perspective, one related more to psychology than physics. The intention to "make sure I make a good swing" is likely to promote mechanical thinking and self-consciousness, both of which interfere with a free-flowing motion. However, if your purpose is to fulfill an image of the ball flying or rolling to a target, the image fills your mind, and your body swings the club with far less interference.

When our intention is to avoid embarrassment or protect against making mistakes, we make what we think is a careful swing and try to guide the shot where we want it to go. This prevents us from making a free, full swing and usually produces a poor shot.

The great champion Bobby Jones considered this his most serious weakness. He found that when he was comfortably ahead in a tournament, he began to fear the embarrassment of not holding his lead. He would try to control his swing to avoid making a mistake. Instead of picking a target, he focused on avoiding hazards. He felt that he would have won far more tournaments (and finished more easily the ones he did win) had he focused on his targets as much when leading as when chasing.

The best target is where we want to send the ball. The best intention is to trust our swing. The best purpose is to enjoy playing the game. Think this way and you'll swing freely, get better results, and enjoy yourself more than ever.

your mind's eye

Clarity is having an image of the full shot that you intend—where the ball is going to come to rest and how it's going to get there. To do this, take all your calculations and planning and transform them into an image. I prefer to use the word "image" rather than "visualization." Image, although still visually oriented, can also include feel and sound.

Many golfers have told me they can't visualize. While it's true that some people are more oriented toward auditory or tactile/kinesthetic sensations, we all have some capacity to see in our mind's eye. More often than not, people think visualization is something more than what they're doing. They think it's supposed to be like seeing a movie. However, it is simply whatever you experience *in your mind's eye.*

During a playing lesson, one golfer three-putted four times on the front nine. We broke for lunch, and he asked for some help on the practice green. I asked, "Do you have an image of the way the putt will roll and go into the hole?"

He said, "I can't visualize. I can't see the line of the putt I want to make."

I said, "I understand. A lot of people can't visualize. That's okay. But if you *could* visualize, what would that putt look like?"

He responded without hesitation. "It would start rolling pretty straight out toward the right, and as it slowed down around halfway to the hole, it would start to break, about a foot toward the left, and go in the front right side of the hole."

I replied, "You did it. The way you 'saw' that is visualizing." He went on to play the back nine without three-putting at all.

The part of the mind that runs the body does so by images. In reactive sports, at the moment of action there isn't time to think before shooting or swinging or throwing. The player just reacts to the image of the target. In golf the ball is just sitting there. No one is trying to block your shot or take the ball away from you. You have plenty of time to think about how you are going to swing at it. (Analogous situations in other sports would be pitching a baseball, shooting a free throw in basketball, serving in tennis, bowling, darts, curling, etc.)

When you establish an image of what you intend to do, the body will fulfill it. That becomes the "target." The clearer the image, the more likely that your body will produce it. Therefore, any conceptual interference or unintended image will negatively affect the chances of a good result. The best results come from actions that are responses to an image of the actual target, so the best swing thought is actually an image, not a conceptual thought.

For the same reason, I don't like talking about how much a putt will break by saying, "It's a right-edge putt." What the golfer means is that she expects the putt to move about two inches from right to left in order to enter the hole in the middle. However, the right edge of the hole is the last image in her mind before she putts. It becomes her target and she pushes the ball out to the right just enough for it to hit that right edge and lip out.

Landry, a first-year touring professional, described a round in which he lipped out six times in the last nine holes. When I asked him how he looked at those putts, sure enough he was thinking of them as right-edge or left-edge putts. He had an image of the edge in mind, and found a way to hit his target. I said, "That shows just how skilled a putter you are. It's not nearly as hard to hit a ball into a cup four inches wide as it is to hit it exactly on the edge. You have to be incredibly precise to do that."

We focused on seeing the ball track into the cup, just a tiny bit right or left of the center. He's lipped out far fewer putts since then, and most of the ones he holes pour into the heart of the cup.

the vividness
of the moment

Sense perceptions are necessary for creative imaging of the shots we intend to play. Our senses collect information that we use to direct our mind and body in executing a golf shot and everything else we do. Therefore, it is very helpful to practice awareness of our sense perceptions and how they are experienced.

Start by sitting upright on a chair, feet flat on the floor, hands resting palm-down on your knees or upper legs. Turn your awareness to your sense perceptions, one by one.* First, without moving your eyes, notice as much as you can of what is in your field of vision. No need to mentally comment on what you notice; just notice. See the colors and shapes. Notice the extent of your peripheral vision side to side, above and below. See what is near and what is far.

After about a minute, direct your attention to what you can hear (leave your eyes open). Listen for any kinds of sounds: traffic, machinery, birds, voices, etc. Notice whether the sounds are near or far, the direction they seem to be coming

---

* To do this with smell and taste, you may need to intentionally introduce objects of these senses, so they are omitted in this description.

from. Again, there's no need for commentary about any of the sounds; just notice them.

Having attended to sounds for a minute or so, switch to focusing on bodily sensations: your seat pressing into the chair, feet pressing on the floor, your hands feeling the cloth (or skin) on your legs, etc. Notice your posture. Notice internal sensations like your heart beating, how your body moves with your breathing, the feeling of the air passing in and out of your nostrils or lips. Just notice without mentally commenting.

You may have observed that as you turned your attention to each of the senses, you became aware of much more than you had noticed before. When you're more aware, you take in more information about your circumstances, which allows you to make better choices about your next golf shot (or any course of action, for that matter). Practicing sense perception awareness also builds your capacity to create vivid images of the shot you intend to produce. The more vivid the image, including sight, sound, and feel, the better your intuitive mind can direct your body to produce it. Ben Crenshaw, one of the all-time great putters, said that when he was really putting well, he could smell the dirt in the bottom of the hole.

When you are focusing on one sense, the others fade into the background. You probably heard fewer sounds when you were paying attention to sights or to bodily sensations. This effect has important implications for dealing with thoughts that distract you during your swing routine. Most people find that when focusing on sense perceptions, there is very little mental chatter happening.

Filling your awareness with sense perceptions prevents the arising of distracting thoughts about past or future results. Sense perceptions can only happen in the present, whereas thoughts are mostly about the past or future. Therefore, thoughts and sense perceptions are mutually exclusive. If you're caught up in thoughts of past or future, you can't be "present" to your sense perceptions. If you're attuned to your sense perceptions, fully present, there's no room for mental chatter about the past or future.

In preparing for a golf shot, the best way to use the power of sense perceptions is to make as vivid as possible the visual, auditory, and/or kinesthetic (bodily sensations or feel) image of the swing and target. When you tune in to the vividness of the moment, your body gets clear instructions on where you intend to go, and your thoughts don't interfere with how you get there.

where is your target?

Do you know where the target is? You probably feel like you do, but what we feel isn't always real.

Here's a way to check your target awareness. On the practice range, tee up a ball. From behind the ball, pick out a target in the distance. Then address the ball with your driver (or the usual club you use off a tee). Now close your eyes. Without moving anything else, take your target-side hand off the grip and raise your arm to shoulder height. Keeping your eyes closed, point with your index finger at where you feel the target is. Then, keeping your arm and hand in that same pointing position, open your eyes and gently turn your head to see where your finger is pointing.

Many golfers are pointing at someplace other than the actual target. What does it mean if you are? Without knowing it, you're fighting with yourself. Having set up with an alignment that is different from where you feel you should send the ball, your swing will become a combination of compensations, trying to go in two directions at once.

If you found a big difference between where you were pointing and the target you intended, you can train your eyes and body gradually to be more in sync. Go to the practice range. Pick your target and address the ball. Do the pointing exercise with eyes closed. Look up to see where you are pointing. Move your arm to point at the target. Look back down, feel where your arm is pointing, and bring a visual image to mind of the target *in that direction.* Then make your swing toward your image of the target. Don't pay much attention to where the ball goes; you will probably feel a bit awkward. Do this over and over again. As you get more comfortable and more in sync, your results will improve.

don't hit it into the lake

When we say to someone, "Don't think of a monkey," the image that comes to mind is a monkey. That's because the word "monkey" refers to something we can perceive, but the word "don't" is purely conceptual. On the golf course, when we say to ourselves, "Don't hit it into the lake," the image that appears in our mind is our golf ball flying toward and splashing into the lake.

Golfers tend to have a negative attitude about themselves after hitting the ball in the place they hoped to avoid. They feel incompetent. I turn the tables on them by telling them how incredibly skilled they must be to be able to mis-hit a shot so precisely that it goes exactly where they pictured it.

It is extremely important to have an image in mind of where we *do* want the ball to go. Thinking about where we *don't* want it to go, the hazard that we want to avoid, sets that negative image in our mind. That image is the message our body responds to and does its best to produce.

Ken, a good amateur golfer, relayed this story about a shot in the Los Angeles City Championship: "I'd been driving the ball well, straight and long almost every time. Before each swing, I had a good image of the ball flying to the spot I wanted it to land, then bouncing and rolling to a stop in the right spot on the fairway. As I set up to one tee shot on the back nine, during my last look down the fairway I noticed a small bunker, well short of my usual landing area, and far to the right edge of the fairway. Unfortunately, that was the last image in my mind. Somehow I managed to top and push my drive so that it bounced and rolled right into that bunker. I don't think I could have landed a ball in that bunker if I'd tried to with a hundred shots!"

be decisive

Once a man wanted to get to a particular island just outside the harbor. He went to the dock and found that two boats moored next to each other were both leaving for the island at the same time, but taking different routes. Not being sure which would be better, he stood with one foot in each boat trying to decide. He still hadn't made up his mind as the boats pulled away from the dock, and still couldn't decide when the boats started to go their separate ways. Not putting his trust in one boat or the other, he didn't get to the island—he just got very, very wet.

We've all had the experience—caught between two choices. It might be a choice about which club to use or how to shape the shot. One of the most common such situations occurs when we're putting. We need to decide whether to play a short sidehill putt firmly and straight at the hole or gently with a break. If we aren't decisive about our choice, if we leave doubt in our mind, the chance of making it is almost nil. As Bobby Locke, one of the all-time great putters, said, "Approaching a putt with doubt in your mind is nearly always fatal."

What usually happens if we haven't settled on one plan? Either we hit it firmly and send the ball through the break and past the hole, or we hit it too softly and the putt falls off below the hole.

Why does this occur? Two aspects of mind are involved: One is the conscious, thinking mind that plans; the other is the subconscious, intuitive mind that coordinates body movements. The "planning mind" sends a message to the "coordinating mind," giving it an image of what the body is supposed to accomplish. But when we haven't made a decisive choice, the "coordinating mind" receives two images. So what does it do? It does its best to combine them, and it's usually a losing combination.

This same confusion happens anytime we haven't really made up our mind, when there's lingering doubt as we're about to swing. Preparing for each shot as well as we can and then making a commitment to one plan is the only way that there's a chance for success. The stroke made with commitment will be far better than one subject to the tensions and hesitations that come from fear and uncertainty.

Being Decisive in Your Routine

Breathe deeply and let any competing thoughts dissolve as the breath dissolves out into the atmosphere. Settle into what you've decided with composure as you enter your routine. As you are about to address the ball, one or two doubt-ridden thoughts may arise. Don't try to chase them away, just step back and wait for them to subside by themselves. Then a moment of openness will be left. In that space, step up and execute your stroke.

bacon and eggs breakfast

A man from town asked an old farmer to be on a citizens' committee that would work on improving the town. The farmer asked, "Do you want me to be involved or committed?"

Puzzled, the man asked, "What's the difference?"

The farmer answered, "It's like a bacon and eggs breakfast. The chicken is involved, but the pig is committed."

Commitment involves believing without a doubt that the plan you've made—the image you have, the club you've picked—is the best one. If you have any doubt whatsoever, you're not really committed.

To be able to commit to a plan, you need to feel that you

can handle whatever the outcome is—you need to be willing to pre-accept whatever the results might be. Prepare for your shot as best you can. Have as vivid an image as you can and settle yourself as much as you can. Then commit to it with body, mind, and heart, like the pig in a bacon and eggs breakfast. That level of commitment to the shot you've planned will leave you feeling that your body and mind are synchronized, letting you swing freely with a minimum of interference from negative thoughts. As a player in one of my clinics said on the putting green, "I think I get it. You pick your line and you go with it, come hell or high water." Then he rolled a fifteen-foot downhill left-to-right breaking putt on the line he picked and watched it track right into the center of the cup.

Commitment doesn't guarantee perfect results, but it will give you the best chance of making the shot as you imagined it. If you were truly committed, you pre-accepted whatever result your swing produced. Since we're not robots, there are variations in the swings of even the most accomplished golfers. We can give ourselves a break and accept the inconsistencies in our swings.

Pre-acceptance is important because golf is a game of percentages. Even Ben Hogan felt that he hit only a few shots each round exactly the way he wanted to. That's why top professionals say that champions often win because they have better misses. You can still score very well with good misses. But your misses won't be very good ones if you don't commit to your shot. Being unaccepting of results, frustrated with shots that come off less than perfectly, makes it that much harder to commit to the next shot.

This approach isn't intended to undermine your optimism. Be 100 percent optimistic about and committed to your shot before you make it, and then 100 percent realistic (and forgiving and kind to yourself) about the results.

more curious than afraid

This is a true story, told by my dear friend Pema Chödrön in her book *Start Where You Are: A Guide to Compassionate Living*. It happened in southern California in the early 1900s.

A Native American man by the name of Ishi, the only surviving member of his tribe, had been hiding on an offshore island for some time. He was discovered and brought to an anthropologist at a nearby college who befriended him and took him under his care. The anthropologist taught him English and many things about the modern world while learning as much as he could about Ishi's tribe and their way of life.

One day the anthropologist wanted to take Ishi to San Francisco. They went with some friends to the station to get the train. As it pulled into the station, Ishi slipped quietly behind a column. As the others were boarding the train, they noticed him peeking around the column and they motioned to him to come along. He slowly came out and climbed aboard with the others.

Later the anthropologist asked Ishi how he enjoyed the train ride. Trains of that era belched smoke and made a lot of noise. Ishi and his tribe thought trains were iron monsters that roamed the countryside and ate people. The anthropologist expressed his surprise that even though he thought the train was a monster, Ishi got on board with little more prompting than a wave from his friends. "How did you have the courage to do that?" he asked.

"Well," said Ishi, "since I was little, I was taught to always be more curious than afraid."

Too often as we are about to break through to a new level of success, fear gets in the way. It could be a fear of failure or a fear of success. If we try our hardest and still don't succeed, we might feel devastated. We might feel that doing our best is still not good enough. If we give in to that fear of failure, we find a way to sabotage our round so that we won't be in the position to fall just short at the end. We succeed in avoiding the anxiety, but we never give ourselves a chance to win.

The fear of success is contained in our projections of what will be expected of us afterward and the fear of not being able to meet those expectations. Again, we often find ways to undermine our success to avoid the anxiety we anticipate.

Like Ishi, we can take an attitude of openness and curiosity about the future regardless of what we might encounter.

Facing challenges this way will help us step through our fears and give ourselves a real chance for success. It's been said, "Life is like a turtle. If you don't stick your neck out, you never get anywhere."

However, stepping into the unknown future can have negative repercussions if the ground isn't properly prepared. The key here is pre-acceptance. You need to settle the issue in your mind that you are making a choice with pre-acceptance of *all* the possible results, both good and bad. If you shoot at a pin near a deep bunker, you have to be willing to accept landing in the bunker as a risk you're willing to take against the chance of having a short putt for birdie.

Without acceptance, your disappointment and frustration when things don't go your way will only make matters worse. Masters and PGA champion Jackie Burke, Jr., said, "Be prepared to scramble right from the start." Take your best shot and be ready to deal with the results. Pre-acceptance means taking the attitude that you can handle whatever results you encounter. This reduces fear of unwanted outcomes, meaning less interference with making a free swing. And that means a higher percentage of good results. If you accept the possibility of having to scramble, you'll find yourself scrambling a whole lot less.

natural commitment

Commitment is part of our nature. We have an inherent capacity for it. In that sense, it's an aspect of basic goodness, an expression of unconditional confidence in action. Commitment could be defined as the extent to which every part of our body is directed toward the same target. Debbie Massey, a two-time British Open Champion, compared commitment in golf to a rider taking a show horse into a jump. "The first thing that goes over the fence is the rider's heart. You stand up to that challenging shot, you put yourself into that shot, and you pour yourself into it confidently. Stand up and commit yourself completely. If you miss it, you miss it certainly. You've done everything you can."*

I was once asked, "How do you teach commitment?" Since commitment is innate, it's not something that can be taught. Commitment is a natural part of any action; with no interference, our bodies and minds are committed to the same target. However, a variety of factors can interfere with commitment. Therefore what needs to be taught is how to remove

---

* In Mona Vold's *Different Strokes: The Lives and Teachings of the Game's Wisest Women*.

the interference, how to remove whatever is keeping the rider's heart from going over the fence.

The greatest interference is fear of unwanted results. Yet that is precisely what we get from a lack of commitment. Being willing to accept whatever results a shot may produce, feeling that we can handle whatever the future holds, removes the interference that comes with fear.

If you have skills in playing recovery shots, you'll feel more confident about handling a wider variety of results. Therefore, one way to reduce fear is to strengthen your short game and other shots that help you scramble effectively.

Acceptance is the key. In preparing for any shot, review all your options and adopt a strategy that minimizes risk and maximizes reward. Take a big mind perspective, seeing that even the worst result won't be the end of the world, and that the shot you've planned is one you've accomplished many times. (If you haven't, you might rethink your strategy.) Finally, remind yourself that a shot played with trust will get better results than one played with doubt. Doubt leads to confusion, anxiety, or both. Trust brings comfort and ease, and that allows you to let go and swing freely.

When the interference of fear is gone, our natural commitment to the action we intend is there. Then we can truly put our hearts into it.

A metaphor for this view is one often used in the Buddhist tradition. On a cloudy day, the sun is not absent; it is merely obscured by the clouds. To experience the sun, we don't need to manufacture a new sun in front of the clouds. When the clouds part, the sun will be there, shining brightly. In the same way, commitment is not something we need to manufacture, not something we need to be taught how to do. When we clear away the clouds of fear, doubt, and hesitation, our natural commitment will shine through.

avoid the anyways

Every golfer has had the experience of setting up to a shot and not feeling completely comfortable with some aspect of it. We might have a vague feeling that something is not quite right, or we might know what's wrong but not bother to do anything about it. In either case, when we "go ahead and hit it anyway," the result is usually terrible. I call that kind of shot an "anyway." Anytime we can reflect on a shot and say, "You know, I knew better," that was an anyway. Think about how many strokes you'd save if you could avoid these shots.

The first step in avoiding the anyways is recognizing them. There are many different types. One commonly occurs when using golf carts. You leave the cart and go to your ball on the far side of the green (or the far side of the fairway when there's a "cart path only" rule) and discover that you have the wrong club for the shot. Rather than go back to the cart, you think, "I'll just hit this club anyway."

Another type of anyway is being "between clubs." You're at a distance that's longer than usual for your seven-iron, but shorter than you would probably hit a six-iron. If you set up to the shot with the seven, it crosses your mind that it might not be enough club. When you have the six in your hand, you feel like you might have too much club. If you don't make a clear choice, you're set up for an anyway. Anytime you feel uncommitted to any part of your planned shot—the club, the line, the shape of the shot—and go ahead with your stroke, that's an anyway.

It's an anyway anytime we go ahead when we're not really ready to start our swing. We might realize that we've made a plan that we don't have confidence in. We might have changed to a new plan but haven't gotten comfortable with it. There might be something that distracts us, like a divot hole or root under our foot, or a leaf just behind the ball. Perhaps we're distracted over a putt because we know the group behind us is waiting in the fairway. We might just feel like something's not quite right, and we're not sure exactly what it is. But if we go ahead before we're ready, we've committed an anyway.

There are lots of other anyways that show up at address. We feel too close to or too far from the ball. We feel the ball is too far forward or too far back in our stance. We feel the ball is teed up too high or too low. We feel our stance is a little too open or a little too closed; we feel we're aimed a little too far to the right or to the left. We feel we're playing too little or too much break on a putt. We might feel unsure about the effect of the uphill, downhill, or sidehill lie we have. You can probably add to the list. If we don't feel quite right, we're about to hit an anyway.

If we sense that something is off, why do we go ahead and hit it anyway? In the golf cart example, it's probably some combination of being too lazy to go back to the cart, not wanting to make others wait, and not wanting to look foolish for having to go get a different club. On the tee, we might feel embarrassed to retee the ball, or, imagining others' impatience, not want to take the time to step back and start our routine over again. The anxiety of a tee shot or trouble shot can make us want to get it over with. In support of these reasons we rationalize going ahead even though we're not completely ready. We might say to ourselves, "I can adjust for this while I swing." More subtly, we might talk ourselves into feeling good about the situation. "I feel a little far away from the ball. No, that's where I should be. It'll let me swing out. Actually, that feels good. Yeah, it does." Sorry, but it's still an anyway—even if you convinced yourself. You can use this as a clear signal: If you're having a conversation with yourself as you're about to swing, you're in trouble.

The final step in avoiding the anyways is to recognize that "hitting it anyway" is a habit you can change. In "Pebbles in the Bowl" you'll find a detailed explanation of a simple but powerful technique for changing this and other habits. The basic approach is this: Without judging or criticizing yourself for doing it, just notice when you do an anyway, mark it down on your card, and let it go. Soon you'll catch your anyways before you do them, recommit to the shot, and get far better results.

Getting Comfortable

It is common to feel uneasy about an unusual stance or shot. This uneasiness distracts us and this distraction will likely cause interference. Instead of going ahead anyway, here's how to get as comfortable as you can.

Take the club you intend to swing and assume the stance you intend to take. Waggle the club a bit, feeling what it will be like to swing from that position. Let your body get used to the way that stance feels. The key to getting comfortable with something new and different is getting used to it. You can even say to yourself, "This is how it will feel when I play this shot." Now go back and start your swing routine. Knowing that you've done everything you could to get comfortable will let you make a more confident swing.

dive under the waves

To deal with last-minute thoughts, those internal conversations about the shot right before you swing, I suggest an approach taken from body surfing. If you want to swim out where the wave starts so you can ride it in, you have to get past the breakers. Fighting through these breakers takes a lot of strength and energy, and more often than not the waves knock you back. To get past a wave, the easiest thing to do is dive under it so that the wave breaks far above you. Under the water it's surprisingly peaceful in contrast to the turbulence above. You avoid the impact of the breaking wave and come up easily on the other side of it.

With thoughts, the same principle applies. We want to be free from nagging thoughts because they distract us from the task at hand: making a smooth, free stroke with only the target in mind. Fighting thoughts is counterproductive. If we're busy fighting thoughts, we're *already* distracted from executing the golf shot. So how do we "dive under the wave"?

First, see the thoughts as moving through the spacious awareness of your mind. It takes practice to treat your thoughts somewhat objectively, to not get caught up in their story lines. As best you can, let them come and go as if they were moving by like waves above you. Then, as you address the ball, feel as if you are diving under the waves of thoughts. Connect with the peaceful feeling of being below the turbulence, direct your attention to your target, and let the stroke happen.

cool, calm, and collected

A vital part of our preparation for a golf shot has to do with alleviating tension from our body. Excessive muscle tension is an obstacle to making a fluid, powerful golf swing. There needs to be just enough tension to maintain our posture and hold onto the club as we swing, but any more than necessary interferes with the flow of the swing.

There's a simple demonstration of the effect of tension on your golf game that you can do anywhere. Take your putter and set up in your putting stance. As much as you can, let the tension in your body dissolve, including arms and hands, shoulders, and belly. Then make a full pendulum-type putting stroke, as you would for a long lag putt. Repeat the stroke, back and forth, a few times. Notice how freely the putterhead moves. Now tense up your shoulders, hands, and stomach. Swing again, intending to make the same stroke. Did you notice how abbreviated the stroke became, especially on the follow-through? The interference from tension in that putting stroke will have a similar effect on every swing you make. As the saying goes, "You don't play golf to relax, you relax to play golf."

The first step in releasing excess tension is recognizing where and how much tension there is in your body. The following exercise includes both a method to identify tension and a gentle technique to dissolve it.

The Body Scan

The body scan is a practice for enhancing awareness of residual tension in your body. It's often done lying flat on one's back (although this sometimes results in falling asleep before one is finished), but it's fine to do it sitting in a chair. Eventually, you'll be able to do a quick version while standing up, out on the golf course.

Direct your awareness to each area of your body, noticing how much or little tension you feel at each point. Start at the top of your head, noticing your scalp, face, jaw, and neck. Then direct your awareness to shoulders, arms, and hands. Scan your torso, being aware of any tension in your chest and upper back, stomach, lower back, deep belly, pelvis, and genitals. Scan down each leg: thighs, knees, calves, feet, and toes.

As you do this the first time, just notice how much tension there is without doing anything about it. Distinguish between the tension necessary to hold your posture and tension that isn't necessary. This is a key distinction that applies to golf. As we said before, we need a certain amount of tension to maintain our posture and hold onto the club. Any more than that interferes with the flow of the swing.

For some people, just noticing it as you scan will dissolve

the excess tension to some extent. If you'd like, you can apply a technique that will reduce tension further. Scan again, either from head to toe or vice versa, this time resting your awareness on an area of your body where you encounter excess tension and imagining that, like snowflakes in the morning sun, the tension melts in the light of awareness. Finally, scan once more, and at any areas where the tension seems to stubbornly persist, imagine that each breath you take flows in and out through that area of your body, as if it is ventilating the tension.

The first few times you practice the body scan, do it slowly enough to become aware of each area of your body. As you get more familiar with the practice, you will be able to do it more quickly. Before long you will begin to intuitively associate awareness with easing of tension, so a brief scan will clear away a lot of unnecessary tension.

Here's how to use the body scan on the golf course:

In practice rounds, do a quick body scan before each shot. Notice which situations give rise to more tension than others, such as the first tee, a tee shot following a bad hole, a shot with hazards in play, etc. Notice which areas of your body hold the most tension. Common areas to find tension buildups are jaws, tops of shoulders (you know, those knots that massage therapists find), hands, and deep belly. By tracking your tendencies, you'll know when in a round to scan for tension and where in your body to look for it. Then use the tension-reducing techniques discussed here to clear away as much tension as you can before you play the shot.

listen to your intuition

Facing a difficult recovery shot is a particular situation that's likely to give rise to an anyway. There's a method to avoid compounding one mistake with another. When you set up as though to play the shot, tune in to your body. Using the body scan, feel how comfortable or uncomfortable you are. You'll intuitively sense the difficulty of the shot you're planning. If you feel like there's little chance for a good result, change plans. With a better risk-reward ratio, you'll likely experience relief and far less tension in your body. Play the shot you feel less anxiety about and keep your scores down.

In "Avoid the Anyways" I mentioned the difficulty of being between clubs. Again, listen to your intuition. Take both clubs and set up to the shot with each, feeling the level of tension in your body. Notice if one club makes you feel uneasy, and if the other gives a feeling of relief and ease. Your body is telling you which club you'll swing with more confidence. Trust your intuition and pick the one that puts your mind and body at ease.

You may find you are distracted and hurrying because the foursome behind you is waiting. Notice if you are taking responsibility even if the group in front of you is slow, or someone else in your foursome is the slow player. Recognize the anxiety you cause yourself even when the situation is not in your control. Rushing through your routine, thinking about the group behind you instead of the shot you're preparing for, is a recipe for disaster. (Often golfers play their worst when they are "playing through" a slower group, hurrying to go by while that group watches.)

If the group in front of you is making you wait, find an opportunity to explain the situation to the group behind you. That might put you more at ease. Finally, here's a thought that will help you to slow yourself down in that type of situation: Taking an extra few seconds over a putt takes less time than a second or third putt. And taking an extra few seconds to properly prepare for a tee shot takes a *lot* less time than looking for your ball in the woods.

center of gravity

In the martial arts and similar mind-body traditions of the East, the body's "center of gravity" is the source from which all movement and energy flow. It is located a few inches below the navel, in the center of the torso. In the Japanese martial arts it is called the *hara,* in Chinese traditions like tai chi it is called the *dantien,* and in Tibetan Yoga it is called the *chöjung.* In each of these systems the practitioner is instructed to direct her awareness to that place. Awareness of this center of gravity is extremely helpful in golf. In the backswing, when we make a good turn away from the target, it is our center of gravity that we coil around. As we make the transition and uncoil, it is the source from which the power of the swing emanates. When we make a good finish, it is our center of gravity that is pointing directly at the target. A common technical instruction is "to finish with your belt buckle pointing at the target." For most people, the belt buckle is a few inches below the navel.

It may come as a surprise, but our state of mind affects our center of gravity. The relationship between mind and body is such that wherever our mind is focused, the center of gravity will shift in that direction. When we're very uptight, thinking a lot, full of chatter in our mind as we enter into a shot, it will be as if our center of gravity is up near our head. How steady a swing would you make with a twenty-pound helmet on your head? You would be much more likely to sway off center, lose your balance, and lunge at the ball. But when you feel grounded, down-to-earth, centered in your body, you are much less likely to sway and lunge.

You can feel the difference through this simple exercise. Take your stance as if you were going to swing a driver, but without a club. Put both hands, one on top of the other, palms in, on your center of gravity, a few inches below your navel. Now move as you would in a golf swing, turning away, then turning back, finishing toward the target. Do this a few times, feeling your balance and how easily you maintain it.

Now put your hands on top of your head. Make the swinging motion a few times and feel your balance. Most likely, you discovered how hard it is to stay centered, how easy it is to sway. You raised your center of gravity by placing your hands on your head.

The second part of the exercise demonstrates how your center of gravity changes with your mental focus. You'll need a friend to help you with this.

Stand upright, with feet shoulder width apart and knees slightly flexed (like a good golf posture). Put your attention on your chest and upper back and feel as if most of the weight of your body is there in your upper torso. As you breathe out, feel that the weight is settling lower in your body, at the level of your ribs. With the next breath, feel that it's settling down in your belly. With the next breath, feel it in your hips. Next, feel it in your upper legs; feel that most of the weight of your body is centered there in your upper legs.

At this point, ask your friend to push lightly against the front of one of your shoulders (make sure there's nothing behind you). You'll feel the shoulder give a bit, but your lower body remains stable.

Then take the same stance, but this time put your attention on your forehead, clench your jaw, and tense the muscles where your shoulders meet your neck. Feel that most of your weight is there on your shoulders, neck, and head.

Ask your friend to give you the same little push in the same spot. It's quite likely that the same push that had little effect on you the last time will make you tip over on your heels and you'll need to step back to keep your balance.

Obviously, nothing physically changed in the actual weight distribution in your body. But there was a clear physical difference based on the change in your *effective* center of gravity created by your mind. Mental chatter along with tension in jaw and shoulder muscles can raise your center of gravity as if you were swinging with your hands on your head.

To ensure a good center of gravity for your swing, it's helpful to take a full "settling" breath behind the ball, just before you approach it and take your stance. Be sure to finish the out-breath completely before you start walking toward the ball. As you breathe out, feel your center of gravity settle below your waist, into the place where you'll generate your full power.

remember to breathe

Let's start with an exercise. Take your golf stance and close your eyes. For a few seconds, think of a situation that you're afraid of or that causes you anxiety when you anticipate dealing with it. Now check on your breathing—is it deep and relaxed? Chances are it isn't. Most people respond that they were barely breathing at all. If there was any breathing, it was constricted and very shallow.

This is a natural reaction. Animals freeze at sounds of danger and stop breathing to better hear what is approaching. In the same way, when we anticipate a stressful situation, we tense up and stop or subdue our breathing. (This exercise works because our body responds to imagined danger as if it were real.)

For the next part of the exercise, take your stance again, close your eyes, and take a few slow, even breaths. Imagine that the breath goes deeper into your body with each inhalation, filling it as much as possible. Now check on your body and mind—is your body tense, your mind filled with anxiety? Not likely. Most people respond that their bodies become more relaxed and their minds feel more at ease, just by experiencing their breath in their bodies.

The point is that tension and deep breathing are incompatible. If you're tense, you won't be breathing deeply; if you breathe deeply, tension dissolves. Dr. Herbert Benson presents this as a method of stress reduction in his book *The Relaxation Response.* By introducing a relaxation-producing behavior (like deep breathing) when confronted with a stressful situation, you begin to train yourself to respond in a different way. Eventually, situations that would ordinarily produce tension and anxiety instead call forth a response of relaxation and steadiness.

How to Breathe*

Few people know what it means to take a full breath. If you watch, most people inhale rapidly and raise their shoulders.

---

* Persons with respiratory issues should consult a health professional before doing any breathing exercise.

That is a hard high breath, but not a full one. Only the tops of the lungs fill up, and the raised shoulders are actually in a position of tension.

Then there is a deep breath, in which you inhale deeply into your torso, filling your lungs to the bottom. Some people call this a belly breath, since filling the bottom of your lungs presses down your diaphragm, pushing out your belly. A deep breath is better than a shallow one, but there is a more complete way to breathe, called a full breath. As human beings, we're very frontally oriented. Eyes, nose, and mouth are all in the front of our face, and even our ears have their opening toward the front. The natural bend in our elbows moves our hands forward for feeling. Most of us have more awareness of our front than our back, and little feeling for the thickness of our torso.

To experience a full breath, sit up or stand with good posture and close your eyes. Breathe gently and slowly through your nose. Feel the breath going down the *back* of your throat. On the next few breaths, feel as if your breath were going into your back, filling it first side to side and then down to your tailbone. You can imagine that your back is like a thin, inflatable camping pad, filling with breath to an even thickness across your whole back. As you breathe gently this way, you'll feel your shoulder blades widen a bit and the back of your rib cage spread wider. Finally, your back will seem to get longer as you feel as though the breath is reaching down to your tailbone. This feeling is excellent for your golf stance, as the widening of your back lets your arms hang more freely, and the lengthening feeling means your back is straighter.

Practice this way of breathing as often as you can, in any setting. Soon it will become your natural way of breathing. Making full use of your lungs is a tremendous benefit. You are providing the maximum amount of oxygen to your blood and through it to your muscles and brain. You'll not only be breathing fuller, you'll be breathing smarter.

Breathing in the Swing Routine

Often golfers find themselves in tension-producing situations without realizing how much they're affected. Therefore, to be sure you remember to breathe and diffuse the tension before executing any challenging shot, I recommend incorporating a full breath into your swing routine for *every* shot. It actually makes an ideal "trigger" for the start of your approach to the ball from behind, which is the beginning of your swing routine.

Stand eight to twelve feet behind the ball, where you can look straight down your aim line. Having engaged your mind fully in the image of the shot you've planned, gently take a full breath through your nostrils and slowly exhale through your nostrils and/or mouth. Only when the exhalation is completed do you start your approach to the ball. This transition from breathing to walking is very important. As explained later in "Transitions," your tempo is established long before you begin the backswing.

I can quite accurately predict the quality of many golfers' shots by whether or not they complete their outbreath before starting toward the ball. When they do, the swing is usually flowing and smooth. When they start toward the ball without waiting for the outbreath to be completed, that rushed quality appears again in the takeaway and in the transition from back-swing to downswing. They usually say, "I got quick," in their explanation of what caused such a poor shot, thinking it happened during their swing when in fact it started much earlier.

A key to the relationship between tension and relaxation is the body-mind feedback loop. The mind not only directs the body, it gets feedback from it as well. So if we confront real or imagined danger, the mind sends a message to the body to tense up. As long as the tension lingers, when the mind checks on the body, it recognizes tension and figures that "we're still in danger." However, if we breathe fully to ease the tension in the body, when the mind checks on the body, it recognizes the lack of tension and concludes that "we're not in trouble any-more." This is a further expression of full breathing and ten-sion being incompatible.

So when you stand up on the first tee, or the shot over the lake, or any shot that might produce apprehension, remember to breathe.

cultivating and
strengthening awareness

In golf, if we keep thinking about a mistake we made on a previous hole, or project how our score will turn out at the end of the round, it's as if we're daydreaming. Our mind is completely filled with images of the past or future. Lacking awareness of the task at hand leads to poor decision-making before the shot and distraction while we're swinging.

We spend much of the time "asleep" to the present moment, preoccupied with thoughts about the past and future. However, our inherent capability to be aware means we can "wake up."

This ability to be aware of all the aspects of our experience can be cultivated and strengthened through practice. Just like muscles that atrophy from lack of use, if we don't use our awareness to its fullest capacity, it becomes dull. It needs to be exercised to keep it sharp. Use it or lose it.

When we cultivate a plant or tree, it requires regular attention. In the same way, awareness requires regular practice. The four parts of this chapter describe the elements of an awareness practice session.*

---

* My two main meditation teachers, the Tibetan master Chögyam Trungpa, and his principal student, Ösel Tendzin, emphasized a combination of mindfulness and awareness practices. Although the practices described in this

The first part, "Taking Your Seat," describes the physical posture that supports your practice throughout the session. "Getting Focused" establishes mindfulness as a foundation for strengthening your ability to concentrate. "Staying in the Present" introduces the method for cultivating awareness, the main practice of the session. As the concluding phase of your session "Expansive Awareness" broadens your horizons and opens you to the experience of big mind.

Taking Your Seat

The first step in cultivating awareness is sitting still. Until we strengthen our awareness, the hustle and bustle around us will continually distract our mind. This is why Shambhala warriors and martial arts practitioners' "basic training" is the sitting practice of mindfulness/awareness.

Begin by finding a place where you can sit alone for a few minutes. Traditionally, awareness practice is done while sitting on a firm cushion several inches thick with legs crossed and feet resting on a mat or carpet. However, you may find it easier to sit on a chair. Sit in the center of the chair, not leaning against the back. Rest your feet flat on the floor.

Good posture is very important. It allows the breath to

---

book are sufficient for application to golf, if one wishes to delve deeper into the Buddhist or Shambhala traditions, it is important to have personal instruction from a qualified teacher. For information about resources for instruction please email: info@mentalgamemastery.com.

flow naturally and makes it easier to stay alert. To find your best posture, begin by letting your tailbone descend and your buttocks settle into the seat of the chair or cushion. There should be a feeling of trusting the seat to support you. Next, from the back of the top of your head, gently extend upward. To get a feeling for this, you can actually reach up, grasp a lock of your hair at that spot, and gently pull yourself up with it. You'll feel your spine become upright but not rigid, and your chin tuck in slightly. As you simultaneously extend gently upward from the top and settle downward from the bottom of your spine, let everything else in your torso relax around that, as if hanging from your spinal column.

Letting your upper arms hang straight down from your shoulders, place your hands palm-down on top of your legs. Let your jaw relax, with your lips just barely closed. Keep your eyes open, looking forward and slightly downward.

This is the same posture you see in pictures or statues of kings and queens in many cultures. You can also see aspects of it in photographs of many championship golfers. It is the posture of a true warrior. Just by taking your seat in this way, you begin to experience a feeling of dignity and confidence.

> When you sit erect, you are proclaiming to yourself
> and the rest of the world that you are going to be a
> warrior, a fully human being.
>
> —Venerable Chögyam Trungpa,
> *Shambhala: The Sacred Path of the Warrior*

Getting Focused

In the Buddhist tradition, the practice for enhancing focus or concentration is called "mindfulness." Awareness is panoramic; mindfulness is one-pointed. We practice mindfulness as the foundation for cultivating awareness.

The point of mindfulness and awareness practice is just noticing whatever arises in our experience, without comment, judgment, or evaluation. It is sometimes referred to as "bare attention." It is simply being, without having to *do* anything about how we're being. Whatever thoughts, feelings, or emotions arise, the practice is to be with them, to feel them without doing anything about them. Instead of running away from or trying to get rid of anything, stay with the thoughts and emotions and look into them. Just staying in the here and now in this way is an expression of bravery.

However, especially for beginners, this isn't the easiest thing to do. That's because we're so used to doing things, filling up the space, keeping busy, keeping entertained. We're so busy doing things and spend so little time simply being that we should probably be called "human doings" instead of "human beings." When we're not doing something we feel bored, and when we feel bored our minds start to wander. Although we intend to pay attention to our experience in the here and now, our minds have a tendency to wander elsewhere. Therefore we need an anchor, a reference point to come back to. That reference point is our breath.

Mindfulness of Breathing*

After taking your seat with good posture, direct your attention to your breathing. Notice the feeling of your torso expanding and contracting, the sensation of the breath flowing through your nostrils. It is important that you don't manipulate your breathing. However your breath flows, whether deep or shallow, short or long, just notice it with bare attention. After a few breaths, you can begin the mindfulness exercise of counting breaths.

In each stage of the exercise, count the breaths mentally (silently). If your mind wanders and you lose count, go back to the beginning and start the count over. You may find that the counting can continue in an "automatic" way while you are involved in thoughts. If you weren't fully there with the breathing, you were wandering. When you realize it, go back to the beginning and start the count over.

Stage 1. Count every inbreath *and* outbreath until you reach 9. After you can reach 9 without getting distracted, count to 18. Increase the count by 9s until you can stay mindful to 72.

Stage 2. For every cycle of breath, in and out, count the outbreath only. (Breathe in and out, 1; breathe in and out, 2; and so on.) Count until you reach 9 mindfully; then increase the count by 9s until you can stay mindful to 72.

---

* Persons with respiratory issues should consult a health professional before doing any breathing exercise.

Stage 3. Count every cycle on the outbreath as above. However, for this part of the exercise count backward, starting with 9. When you can do that mindfully, count backward from 18, and so on until you can count backward from 72 to 1 without being distracted.

After you have trained in mindfulness practice, you can apply it on the golf course. There will be times when you have to wait for the group ahead, or you are the last one in your group to putt. Breath-counting during those times is especially valuable. It helps you pass the time without getting distracted by thoughts or worries, which are usually about the past or future ("Will I slice it again like I did last hole?" "If I miss this putt, will we lose lose the match?" etc.). Without worries we naturally feel more at ease. When the fairway is clear, or it's your turn to putt, you'll be more settled, present, and able to focus on the task at hand.

Mindfulness of Walking

You can practice mindfulness in another way on the golf course while you're playing. As you walk between shots, direct your awareness to the feeling of your body. In particular, focus on your feet and legs, as they "lift, swing, place; lift, swing, place," and so on. Feel the ground as you walk. If you become distracted, simply return to your awareness of walking. When you arrive at your ball, you'll feel down-to-earth and ready to get on with the business of playing your shot.

Practicing mindfulness of breathing and walking will

strengthen your ability to stay focused and in the present. This will give you a firm foundation for cultivating awareness.

Staying in the Present

Having practiced mindfulness of breathing, we can use it as a transition into awareness. Begin as you did for counting breaths, with good posture, noticing your torso expanding and contracting, the sensation of the breath flowing through your nostrils. Then do a few minutes of counting your breaths.

To begin awareness practice, you stop counting. As you exhale, simply let your awareness follow the breath out. Again, do not manipulate your breathing in any way. Just let your awareness "ride" each breath as it goes out into the space in front of you. As best you can, let your awareness be with the outbreath. This is called mixing mind and breath.

As your breath goes out, it diffuses and dissolves, merging with the space in the room. In the same way, as your breath goes out, let your awareness open up and expand into the space. This is called mixing mind and space. At the point when the outbreath is finished, your mind is open and aware. Rest in that open space, simply being aware. There's no need to follow your breath back in as you inhale. Trust that it will take care of itself. As the next outbreath starts, mix your mind with that breath and ride it into spacious awareness. Continue in that way, using the breath as a reference point for staying in the present.

Working with Thoughts

Golfers who want to "clear their minds" sometimes become frustrated when doing awareness practice because they don't seem to be able to stop their thoughts. This is based on common misconceptions about presence, clarity of mind, and meditation. They think the goal is to be able to make their mind go blank. Unless you're unconscious, that doesn't happen. Your mind will always be full of the contents of awareness, and often those contents will be thoughts. Awareness practice is intended to make you understand the nature of your mind and your thoughts. As we discussed earlier, realizing that "you are not your thoughts" helps you to be able to work with them.

When thoughts come up, just let them come and go as best you can. Notice them without comment, as if you were simply watching them or listening to them. Be an observer rather than identifying with and getting involved in the thoughts.

Although you intend to just watch them, at some point a thought will arise that captures your attention and distracts you, causing you to wander from your practice of mixing mind with breath and space. When you realize you've gotten caught up in the thought and created a string of associations, following them into the past or future, gently bring your attention back to awareness of your breathing and your posture. Simply make a mental note, "thinking" or "wandering," and come back to being with the breath. Whenever the next outbreath starts, mix your mind with it and open out into the space before you. It is important not to evaluate or judge yourself on how often you get distracted. Just acknowledge what occurred and gently bring your attention back to the breath.

When you begin this practice, do it for a few minutes at a time. As you become accustomed to it, you can do it for a little longer, and continue to extend the sessions little by little, for as long as you'd like.

As you practice mixing mind, breath, and space, you develop a very clear awareness of how strong your tendency is to wander into the past or future, and an appreciation for what you are experiencing in the present moment. Gradually your awareness becomes more stable and continuous. You are distracted less often; when there is a distraction, you come back to the present more easily. Whether on the golf course or in any other activity, the more you are able to stay in the present, the better you'll be able to accomplish your intentions.

Expansive Awareness

Expansive awareness is the last phase of a session of mindfulness/awareness practice. Begin your session by establishing your posture and getting focused with a few minutes of counting breaths. Then spend most of the time cultivating awareness by mixing mind, breath, and space. You'll finish with a few minutes of expansive awareness.

For this practice, raise your gaze to look straight ahead or slightly upward. As you exhale, expand your awareness outward in all directions. First let your awareness expand beyond your body into the space around you. As you breathe out again and again, extend farther and become aware of the space in the whole room, in front of you, behind you, and to each side.

Feel that your awareness is expanding beyond the building you're in, outward to the landscape of the city or countryside. Each time you breathe out, feel your awareness opening outward more and more in every direction until it extends all the way to the horizon.

Finally, expand your awareness beyond the horizon, opening out all the way to the sky and beyond it into space. Rest in that feeling of complete openness and awareness for as long as it lasts. Notice the freedom from anxiety, the lack of mental chatter, when you're resting in that expansive awareness.

With practice, you'll eventually be able to expand your awareness into a spacious openness in just a few breaths. Being able to do so is very useful on the golf course (and anywhere else where you might need to ventilate the situation). In life as in golf, you give it your best shot when you're free of tension and self-consciousness. For example, when you have a difficult tee shot or short putt and you're waiting your turn, it's not very helpful to stare at it, think about it, and let your mind get very small. Instead, look up and breathe out, opening to expansive awareness. When it's your turn, you'll be in a much fresher, open, and settled state of mind.

ACTION

The second stage of the PAR Approach is action. The ideal state of mind for action is confident, focused, and in the flow, with body and mind synchronized in the present moment. This allows you to execute a shot free from the interference of mental chatter or paralysis from analysis. Turn over control of the shot from your thinking mind to the intuitive mind that runs your body, stay in the present, and trust your swing. The key point to remember is, take care of the process and the results will take care of themselves.

how to get from the practice tee to the first tee

One of the challenges faced by all levels of golfers is expressed in this lament: "Why can't I hit it on the course the way I was hitting it on the range? It feels so frustrating!"

There are many reasons, all of which tell us a lot about our state of mind on the golf course. Let's start with purpose: What are we trying to accomplish when we hit balls on the range before a round?* It usually has to do with getting comfortable with the swing, seeing how it feels that day, looking for some swing key, and so on.

Once we're on the tee, we usually have a very different purpose. It is about performance: hitting a good golf shot, avoiding making a mistake, and making a good impression on the people watching, especially our playing partners. With such different purposes, it's not surprising that we make different swings on the first tee than we did on the range.

Another difference is consequence. On the range, if you hit a shot that doesn't go where you expect it to, there's no penalty. You rake another ball over and try again. However, you don't get to do that on the golf course. The only time you

---

* Try to avoid working on your swing in a warm-up session. Do it in a *practice* session after the round or on another day.

replay a shot from the same spot on the golf course is when there *is* a penalty involved (lost ball, out-of-bounds, etc.). Fear of making a mistake introduces tension. The possible consequence of not meeting expectations—our own or those we imagine others have of us—also creates tension that we didn't feel on the range. Tension interferes with our tempo and the freedom with which we swing.

Hitting the same club from the same spot over and over until you "get it right" doesn't necessarily mean you've found your swing. You may be making subtle compensations to get the ball to go where you want it to, with that club, from that spot. When you get to a different setting, especially the first tee, that special version of your swing may not work so well.

Often we don't use our complete swing routine on the practice tee. We just set up and hit, then rake another ball over and hit, rake and hit, usually without a specific target. When we get to the first tee, it's very different. Now we have a place we want to send the ball, and we need to aim and address the ball. That's a totally different way of starting the swing.

For all of these reasons, using our swing routine at least at the end of our warm-up session, with different clubs, specific targets, and good images, will give us our best chance for a successful transition to the golf course. Also, understanding the factors that make the first tee different, we can *accept* that our swing may not be exactly the same as on the range, and therefore not feel so frustrated by a less-than-perfect shot. Give yourself time to warm up to the course, no matter how well things went on the practice tee.

Willie was a tour veteran who wanted to tune up his game. As I watched him hit balls on the range, one nice drive after another, I said that those shots looked just fine. He said, "It's easy to get into a rhythm on the range. But it's different out on the course." Later on we looked at some of his past rounds. He often struggled a bit through the early holes, then started to play better. We agreed that he was a "rhythm player," and I suggested how he might get out of his "range rhythm" and into his "course rhythm" before he got on the course.

The rhythm you develop on the range happens while you're hitting shot after shot with the same club from the same spot, often to the same target. On the course it's completely different, almost never hitting the same club twice in a row from the same spot. It takes time to switch from the practice-range rhythm to the playing rhythm.

Almost all tour pros warm up their full swing before a round in a similar way. They hit a few balls with each club, starting with wedges and working their way up from short irons to long irons to fairway woods and finally the driver. Then they hit a few partial wedge shots to finish. I asked Willie to try something different: play a few imaginary holes at the end of his warm-up.

To do this, picture the first hole (or any hole on the course). Create the imaginary boundaries of the fairway using flags on the range. After hitting a tee shot, determine how far you'd be from the green. Picture the green out on the range and play an iron for an approach of that distance. You can include a pretend par-5 and hit driver, three-wood, wedge. For a pretend par-3, tee up the ball and hit a long iron.

Concluding your pre-round warm-up this way will make you feel as if you've already played a few holes when you get to the first tee. You'll feel as if you're already in the rhythm of the golf course.

Willie has included "playing a few holes" on the range in his warm-up and goes to the first tee in playing rhythm. His scores on the first few holes of a round have improved considerably, including one round in which he birdied the first six holes.

transitions

> Watch out for the transitions. They are times of danger, when the present situation is ending and the next situation hasn't yet begun. Those gaps are the places where awareness can most easily be lost. It's like going through a doorway. If you barge through without caution, you open yourself to disruption on the other side. In fact, you invite chaos.
>
> —Vajra Regent Ösel Tendzin

When we use the word "transition" with regard to the golf swing, most people think of the transition from backswing to downswing. However, several other transition points in the swing are of equal if not greater importance.

There is, of course, a transition from the practice tee to the first tee. Then there is the interval between one shot and the start of planning for the next. It's helpful to make this a distinct transition, not letting conversation or extraneous thoughts get in the way. Finish what you're doing, clear the deck, and focus on the task at hand. Go through the factors you need to consider and make your plan. Clear any doubts and commit to the plan.

The next transition is one of the most challenging. Having made your plan with the thinking, conscious aspect of mind, you need to turn over control for the execution of the shot to the intuitive, subconscious mind that runs your body. You play your best golf when you plan with your head, then play from your heart. There are two keys to success in making this transition: (1) filling your mind with a vivid image of the shot you intend to play and (2) settling down—clearing away tension and feeling the center of gravity in your body. To do this, you can use a full breath just before you begin your approach to the ball.

The Swing Routine

The golf swing doesn't start at the takeaway. The swing begins when you're ready to approach the ball. That's why I prefer to call it a *swing routine* rather than a pre-shot or even pre-swing routine. Your tempo at the start of your approach sets the tempo for your swing. Completing the settling breath is essential for a proper transition into the approach. If you start walking toward the ball before you finish your breath, you'll likely start your takeaway before you're set and start your downswing before you finish your backswing.

Having taken your stance, you encounter the transition into the takeaway. Golfers deal with this transition in many different ways. Some start the takeaway before you expect it; others have you wondering if they'll ever do it. What do you do after your last look at the target? Advice on this topic ranges from "wait until you feel ready" to "don't delay an instant after you look back at the ball." The key here is to stay in your tempo. It's different for everyone, so only you know what feels best.

This is not the time to rush. You need to feel set, clear of distracting thoughts, ready to swing from your center of gravity. Like finishing the breath before starting the approach, finish the setup before starting the takeaway.

The other mistake in this transition is taking too long, breaking the flow, inviting tension and uncertainty. If, for whatever reason, you realize that you have been in the address position overly long, do what a baseball player would do. When a batter is facing a pitcher who is taking a long time, at a certain point he'll start to feel "stale," out of the flow. So he steps out of the batter's box. He takes a time-out, then starts his routine again, digging in, getting set, staying loose and in motion.

If you find yourself out of the flow as you're set up over the ball, step out of the batter's box. Give yourself a time-out to restart your routine. Go back behind the ball and begin your approach. Billy Casper, one of the all-time great champions, used to go so far as to put the club back in the bag and start over from there. (I wouldn't recommend going to this extreme for weekend golf. It's important to go through your routine properly, but it's also important to avoid causing undue delay for your playing partners and the groups behind you.)

The impact of this transition point is most noticeable in putting. Golfers struggling with their putting sometimes freeze, feeling unable to start the putter back for fear of making a bad stroke (or the yips) when they bring it forward again. This is caused by a preoccupation with the future, the results. The remedy is developing and committing to a routine, one with a flowing tempo, that you feel will give you the best chance of fulfilling your intention. Focus totally on the routine, and thoughts of results are less likely to imperil any of your transitions.

The transition at the top, from backswing to downswing, determines much of how you will strike the ball. However, it is not one that most of us can do anything about *while* we're swinging. Since your tempo is established earlier in your swing, you can best care for your transition at the top by making good transitions through the swing routine to that point.

The next transition happens at the end of the swing. We transition from actor to observer, sometimes commentator, and all too often critic. In brief, the more awareness and less judgment that takes place in this transition, the better. It's important to reinforce positive results rather than negative ones. The reverse is so often true: We take a good drive for granted but get emotionally distraught over a missed fairway. When we make a good transition from the end of the swing to the start of our walk down the fairway, we establish a positive pattern for later shots.

The final transition is the passage into the time between shots. Making this transition properly means letting go of the past, but not jumping ahead to the future. Remember, "The past is history, the future's a mystery. Being alive in this moment is a gift—that's why they call it the present." Whether it's between shots, between holes, or between rounds, don't forget to smell the flowers along the way. This is the most important transition, because it is only in the present that we can connect with our nature of basic goodness and simply appreciate being alive.

synchronizing body and mind

When body and mind are synchronized for a golf swing, they are unified in purpose, presence, and focus. They are functioning in the same place at the same time.

Can you send your body into the past or the future? Do you have a time machine? Of course not. Our body is in the present and only in the present. Can you send your mind into the past or the future? Of course you can. (In fact, we spend most of our time in the past or the future, thinking about what happened before and wondering—or worrying—what's going to happen next.) But the mind can be in the present as well. Therefore, the only way our body and mind can be synchronized is if our mind is in the present.

Further, although our mind may be in the present, is it in the same *place* as our body? Most of us have been in the situation of being the last one to putt on a hole, looking back and seeing the foursome behind us standing in the fairway, waiting. If you missed your putt, there's a good chance it was because your body was on the putting green but your mind was back in the fairway with the group behind you. If your mind is anywhere but "in your body," then body and mind are out of sync. This goes for any swing you make on the golf course and any action you undertake anywhere else in your life.

There are situations that seem to be synchronized but actually are not. Your mind can be in the present, thinking about your swing, and yet not be synchronized with your body. The key point here is "thinking about." If you're thinking *about* your swing, you're thinking, not swinging. Your mind is "in your head" with conceptual ideas about how you *should* swing, rather than "in your body," running the swing. If mind and body are doing two different things, they're not synchronized.

Worrying about how a shot will turn out can also interfere with synchronization of body and mind. When I mention this as an obstacle, some golfers ask what the difference is between that concern for the results and having an image of the full shot going to the target. Although an image of the ball flying toward the green includes an intended result, the image is an expression of a positive intention rather than a negative expectation.

Concern about what the result will be is different from envisioning a result you intend. There is no tension in having an image, and an image of a good shot actually reduces tension. Worry, on the other hand, creates an entirely different feeling in the body and a different focus for the mind. It can lead you further into the future. You may anticipate how you'll feel if you get the result you hope for or the result you fear. That makes you think about what you'll have to do next, how it will affect your score, etc. The body hasn't hit the shot yet, but the mind is already in the future, so body and mind are clearly not synchronized.

During a round at Qualifying School, one of the players I was watching missed three consecutive three-foot putts for par on the first three holes, then lost his temper and snapped his putter over his knee.

For the rest of the round, he putted with his driver. Given that he was 3 over par after three holes and putting with his driver for the next fifteen, what do you think he shot for the round? Eighty? Eighty-five?

In fact, over the next fifteen holes, he made only one bogey, sank several par-saving putts, and rolled in five birdies to finish at 71, 1 under par for the round.

In several rounds previous to this one, he hadn't made five birdies with his putter. And he certainly hadn't practiced putting with his driver. So what happened?

Up to this point, a lot of factors were interfering with his putting. He was remembering all the putts he'd missed recently, so now he looked at his putter as the thing he missed putts with. Being a pro who'd played on the PGA Tour, he had lots of expectations that he *should* make all those short putts and more of the long ones. He felt that others expected him to make them, too. Finally, there was the pressure of playing with his career on the line. His perspective had become one of trying to hole putts instead of trusting his stroke.

All of this made him focus more on whether or not the ball would go in the hole (the future) than on his putting routine (the present). His body and mind were completely out of sync. However, when he had to putt with his driver, there was no idea that he *should* make any of the putts. There were no expectations and thus there was no pressure. Since he hadn't practiced putting with a driver, he had to pay full attention to the process—keeping the face of the club square to the line and putting a good stroke on the ball. All he could do beyond that was pick the best line he could and trust his intuition for the feel that would give him the best pace. His body and mind were synchronized in the moment and the process. And the putts kept going in.

In a conversation a few weeks later, we discussed what had happened that day. I described what I felt made him putt so well with his driver, and suggested he try taking that attitude with his putter. Instead of worrying about whether he would hole the putt, he would focus on picking a line, trusting his feel, keeping the face square to the line, and making a good stroke. He said that made sense and he'd give it a try. He called the next evening to let me know how the round went. He had made nine birdies.

give it time to sink in

As we address the ball, occasionally something happens that makes us want to change our mind. It may be a change in the wind, something about our lie or stance that we didn't notice before, or an uneasy feeling about our club selection. When you change your mind about how you're going to play a shot just before you execute it, there's more that needs to be done than you might think.

When you change your mind, you need to leave time for two things to happen. First, your mind has to get comfortable with the new idea. Clear away any lingering thoughts about the old plan. You need to be completely committed to the new one. However, commitment isn't only experienced in the thinking mind. It's also felt in the body. Your body has to feel comfortable with the new plan.

For your body to shift to the new plan, the message has to get from the thinking side of your brain to the side that controls your motor coordination. Too often I've seen a top player change his mind, go directly into a shot, and mess it up.

His mind has changed to a new plan, but his body is still operating on the old one. Out of sync and out-of-bounds.

I saw a vivid illustration of this at the PGA Tour event at Riviera Country Club in Los Angeles one year. A top international player was just off the green with a tricky chip down a slope to the hole. He stood there for quite a while making about a dozen practice swings with one of his wedges. Then he shook his head and exchanged the wedge for a different one. He took two quick practice strokes and addressed the ball. I thought, "That wasn't enough time after changing plans. This will be trouble." Sure enough, he bladed the chip across the green.

He hadn't given the new plan time to sink in. Although his thinking mind had switched to the new plan, his body was still running on the old image. It takes time for a message to get from one side of your brain to the other.

If you change your mind, you need to give your body time to get to where your mind is. It can take up to ten seconds. After you make a new plan, take a few warm-up swings with the new image in mind and allow enough time to let it sink in. Then you can flow through your routine with body and mind in sync and fire away with confidence.

never keep more than a hundred thoughts in your mind during your swing

Everyone agrees that when we have a lot of thoughts while swinging, poor results follow. Why wouldn't we want to be thinking during our swing? Why wouldn't thinking help our body to do what our mind wants it to do?

To understand this dynamic, we need to understand different aspects of mind and how they relate to the action of our body swinging a golf club. The many expressions of mind can be described in various ways. There are thoughts, feelings, perceptions, and emotions. There are big mind and small mind, conscious and subconscious, left-brain and right-brain, analytical and intuitive. These are all aspects of one mind. There aren't two minds or three or four. However, talking about different minds can be helpful in understanding different manifestations. They are like facets of a jewel, showing different qualities. Each provides a window into the essence of mind. For our golf game it's helpful to talk about three facets: thinking mind, intuitive mind, and critic mind.

Thinking Mind

Thinking mind operates by using concepts and words. It analyzes and calculates. It sorts through the information that comes in from the senses and internal feelings, comparing it to information remembered from past experiences. Thinking mind does an excellent job of synthesizing all this information into a plan for action. In golf the thinking mind analyzes information about distance, lie, wind, humidity, and past experiences. It calculates risk versus reward. It makes decisions and plans.

This aspect of mind thinks about what is happening in the environment. It also thinks about what is happening in our body and our thoughts. That's what we call self-consciousness. It's important to understand that this is not simple awareness, or what we've called "just noticing." Self-consciousness is thinking *about* our experience. To think about something implies a quality of separation, in the same way that looking *at* something requires some separation between observer and object. We may even feel like our thinking mind is in our head, watching our body. That's why when we're thinking about our swing, body and mind are not synchronized. Body is swinging, but mind is thinking about swinging and therefore separate from it.

Intuitive Mind

Intuition is a kind of knowing without thinking or analyzing. Intuitive mind directs the body without conceptual thoughts. Imagine how difficult life would be if we had to think about every movement we make. Intuitive mind is the basis of habits. Once we've learned a sequence of movements through repetition, we don't need to direct each step consciously. What's referred to as "muscle memory" isn't in the muscles; the memory is in intuitive mind.

Intuitive mind functions as "bare" awareness: It gathers the experiences of the senses without adding concepts or judgments. Because intuitive mind is nonconceptual, it is never in the past or future but always present and always connected to the body. Therefore, when the intuitive mind is in control, body and mind are synchronized. When we're mainly in the mode of thinking mind, self-consciousness interferes and body and mind are not synchronized. Golfers know how self-defeating that is.

Intuitive mind can direct muscle movements in very subtle increments. When the thinking mind tries to run the body, it does a very bad job. This is because it only uses concepts, which are general categories, like "harder" or "softer." It's like giving someone directions without being able to use anything shorter than miles. If a turn is two and a half miles ahead, you can only say "two miles" or "three miles." In either case someone would miss it by a half-mile. The same applies to golf. If our thinking mind is in control as we're about to putt, and it directs the body with the thought "Hit it hard enough," the ball goes six feet past the hole. When we trust our intuitive mind to run our body, we have a much better touch around the green.

There's a story that a worm asked a centipede how it moved all those legs in the right order. As soon as the centipede thought about it, it got all tangled up and couldn't move. In golf that's called paralysis from analysis. Golfers describe themselves as thinking about so many things to do (or not to do) that they feel mentally twisted up like a pretzel.

This doesn't mean we should reject the thinking mind. It's essential for analyzing the situation, making calculations, and selecting appropriate strategies. However, when it comes time to execute the shot, we need to make a transition. We need to picture a clear image of the ball traveling to the target, then let intuitive mind take over. That's why the best prescription is, "Plan with your head, then play from your heart."

Critic Mind

A third facet of mind is critic mind. It is a special function of the thinking mind. It evaluates, judges, and gives descriptions in terms of good and bad. This aspect of mind is a necessary part of the learning process. Evaluating the results of our actions provides feedback for the thinking mind to make the next plan and for the intuitive mind to make subtle adjustments in body movements. However, the critic mind becomes our own worst enemy when it goes beyond constructive feedback and becomes linked with negative emotions. According to our critic mind, when the results of our actions don't live up to expectations (our own or ones we think others have of us), we should feel bad. So we do.

A problem with the critic mind is that it has tunnel vision. It can focus on one thing that seems wrong, missing all the rest of the picture that's right. In golf the critic mind introduces negative self-talk and self-doubt. Soon we don't trust ourselves. It would be far more helpful to allow for mistakes without judging ourselves so harshly. If we trust that our nature includes awareness and the capacity to learn and grow, the critic mind can provide information without judgment, and we can rely on our intuitive mind to adjust and evolve in the direction we intend.

There is a way to use the tunnel vision of the critic mind to benefit our golf game. We can direct it to look for a positive element in whatever action we do. During a lesson a beginning golfer was very critical of her shots going off-line, and began to feel very frustrated and discouraged. I encouraged her to direct her critic mind toward a positive aspect of each shot. As an example, after she made a swing I said, "That one had a great sound, really crisp." By focusing on the sound instead of the results, in a few shots her whole mood changed. She was hitting lots of crisp shots and more were going on her intended line. After hitting the last ball in her bucket, she turned and said, "Didn't that one sound great!"

during your swing is not the time to give yourself a lesson

Players often rely on swing thoughts, but as we discussed earlier, thinking while swinging isn't such a good idea. It's preferable to have a swing image, one that includes at least the path and finishing point of the ball, but can also include the feel of the swing.

For players who need a swing thought, it is better to have one that describes *what* you intend to do rather than *how* you intend to do it. For example, the thought "long arms" gives an image of *what* you want to feel. However, "extend the arms" gives direction about *how* you want to move. It invites the thinking mind to try to direct the body, which doesn't work very well. Swing thoughts with an image of a feeling allow the intuitive mind to direct the body.

Lessons on the golf swing often include a prescription for the repetition of specific movements until they are incorporated into the swing. Not many weekend golfers, however, have the time or inclination to work on their swings until the new movement is grooved before they go out to play on the course. They use a mental instruction in that movement as their swing thought for the round, which leads to mechanical and self-conscious thinking during each swing. And that's not the time to give yourself a lesson.

The Programming Swing

Here's a technique you can try instead. You can best incorporate a move you've been practicing into your swing during play if you focus on it *before* you swing rather than thinking about it *while* you swing. Having planned your shot and selected your club, stand behind the ball near the spot where you'll start your swing routine. You're going to make a programming swing. Produce the specific movement you want to make. You don't have to make a full swing or swing at full speed. It's more effective to move in a way that allows you to be aware of your body and your club. It may be helpful to close your eyes while doing this, to give your intuitive mind a feel for what you want your body to do. After swinging this way a few times, tell yourself that the move is "programmed in." It's as if your body is a computer, and once you've programmed it, you just let it run. You don't have to keep checking to see if it's still on the program. Naturally, the more you've practiced, the better your body will incorporate the move you've programmed.

Having made your programming swings, there is no longer any need to think about that move. Stand behind the ball, get your image of the shot to the target, take and release a full breath, and walk up to address the ball. Trust your intuitive mind to do its best to include the "programmed" move, and swing away.

give up control
to get control

This is one of the many paradoxes of golf. The control we want to get refers to consistent accuracy, control over where the ball will go. The control we have to give up is the kind we exercise when we "steer" a shot. Steering is an expression of the thinking mind trying to control the swing to *make sure* we get the results we want. Paradoxically, the results we get usually range from not very good to terrible. To get control that leads to consistent accuracy, you have to give up that conscious, intentional type of control: your thinking mind trying to direct your muscles.

Here's a little exercise that will help you differentiate between the two types of control. On a blank sheet of paper, sign your name the way you would a letter or a check, but very large. Now, starting at the beginning, *slowly and carefully* trace directly over the line of your signature for about the first half of it. *Be careful not to go off the line. Watch what you're doing. Do not make a mistake.*

Okay, how did you do? Did you feel less relaxed and at ease when tracing than you did when just signing your name? Were you gripping the pen more tightly? Almost everyone's tracing comes out jerky and jagged and uneven. Which would you like your golf swing to be more like, the first signature or the traced one? Our signatures have smoother lines and a lot more flow to them when we just sign our names than when we try to be careful not to make a mistake. Flow is seriously impeded when we try to consciously control the movements of our muscles. That type of control arises when we try to protect ourselves from things going wrong. The ego-centered, self-conscious thinking mind is what needs to give up control.

How can giving up control lead to *getting* control? Have you ever hit a shot when it felt like "you" weren't running the swing, when it felt almost effortless, with no thoughts about how to swing the club or trying to make it come out a particular way? Most golfers have, if only rarely, had that experience. The results usually range from great to spectacular, and it illustrates how effective it is to give up control. It feels as if we've given up control, because we tend to identify with our thinking mind. However, we haven't actually lost control. We've just transferred it.

The intuitive mind is what gets control. It's the expert at running the body, and it exerts beautiful control over the tiniest muscle movements if it is not interfered with by the thinking mind.

Most of us have seen a waiter in a restaurant carrying a tray full of bowls of soup. He is looking where he's going, not at the tray of soup. Imagine such a scene in which his boss comes over to him and says, "Watch what you're doing. Watch those bowls of soup and be extra careful. Make sure you don't spill the soup." There would be soup all over the place. We all know what it feels like when we're overly careful, watching what we're doing, trying to avoid making a mistake. It usually invites just what we're trying to avoid.

Tim is an assistant pro who really connected with the metaphor of the waiter and the soup. The day after our session, I got a call about how his round had gone. He said he shot 43 on the front nine, then realized that the whole time he'd been "watching the soup." He decided to give up that kind of control and shot 33 on the back nine.

you produce what you fear

"You produce what you fear" is one of my favorite sayings. It applies on many levels, in golf and in life. Let's take some examples from the golf course. In "Don't Hit It into the Lake," we talked about being afraid of hitting the ball into the lake. Fear made that image completely fill our mind. Then our body did a great job of fulfilling the image and we produced what we feared. Splash!

On the psychological level, fear produces the tendency to overcontrol. The thinking mind takes over, and our movements are marked by self-consciousness. We are overly cautious and hesitant. If we're afraid of missing the fairway, we try to steer the shot, make an awkward swing, and the ball heads for the rough. We produced what we feared.

On the physical level, fear produces certain bodily reactions. This is described in stress studies as the fight-or-flight syndrome. Our systems are geared to freeze and stop breathing when we have fear, like a deer in the headlights. The blood flows to our big muscles (as if getting ready to run from a saber-toothed tiger), so we lose sensitivity in our hands and make poor decisions with our brain. Adrenaline flows freely, so we get speedy and jumpy. The muscles get tense, interfering with any chance of making a full turn, a full extension at impact, or a full release. If we fear hitting a bad shot, our body is in a state that will very likely produce what we fear.

One example of this is being afraid of hitting a pull hook out-of-bounds or into a hazard. There is a fear of going left (for right-handers). As we start our downswing, our body naturally starts to turn to the left. But that's where we didn't want to go. Fear makes our body freeze, restricting the turn. However, our arms continue to swing and wrap around our body. The result: a pull hook. We produced what we feared.

Another thing we fear is loss of self-esteem, a feeling of low self-worth. We fear feeling bad about ourselves. We also fear our own self-punishment (berating ourselves for a bad shot). This fear might be based on our own standards for performance. We are afraid we won't "measure up." Often it involves fear of what others might think of us. This is usually mistaken thinking—rarely do others think of us as critically as we think they do. If we attach our self-worth to the results of a golf shot, then missing an "easy" putt of four feet on the last hole is something of which we are extremely fearful. There is heightened tension that interferes with our stroke, and we produce what we fear.

How do we avoid the self-fulfilling prophecy of producing what we fear? We can't deny our fears; that would be false confidence. Rather than trying to get rid of fear, we can learn to go beyond it. That is true fearlessness.

The first step toward going beyond fear is acknowledging it. We can recognize our fears and learn to choose how we respond rather than automatically react to them. A fundamental practice of Shambhala warriorship is directing awareness toward what we fear. Within the space of awareness, we can get a big mind perspective on what we fear. We can take a step back and see a moment on the golf course as one moment out of many in our life. As U.S. Open champion Dr. Cary Middlecoff said about losing a tournament, "It's not life-and-death. My wife will still love me and my dog won't bite me when I get home."

With perspective comes insight. We can see what's behind our fears and the extent to which we tie our self-worth to results. That kind of insight changes our experience of the situation. When fearlessness takes us beyond fear, we can accept the possibilities of both good and bad results without taking them as measures of our self-worth. It's fine to take your golf seriously, but don't take yourself seriously.

Once we've recognized a fear and put it in perspective, we need to undo its effects before executing the shot. Take the time to breathe fully to counteract the excess tension in your body. Clear your mind of any negative images of what you *don't* want to happen, replacing them with positive images of what you *do* want as the outcome. Then body and mind are synchronized and focused on the shot at hand, without the interference of fear.

hitting the target
ten thousand times in a row

Do you think you could hit a target ten thousand times in a row? Your answer is probably similar to that of most of the participants in my golf schools, who shake their heads and say, "No way."

Well, when was the last time you missed your mouth with your fork when you were eating? In the past few months you have hit your target at least ten thousand times in a row. Each time you took a forkful of food, I doubt you were saying to yourself, "Keep your elbow close to your side. Keep your wrist cocked. Keep your head still." You don't consciously direct your arm and hand every time you take a bite of food. You don't think about mechanics while you're using your fork, but you never seem to miss your mouth.

We discussed this one morning and all got a big laugh at lunch that day. One of the participants exclaimed, "I was thinking about how I used my fork to put food in my mouth and I missed!"

Here is the point: You don't need to consciously direct

your body for it to hit a target accurately. Consciously thinking about how you perform a physical activity interferes with doing it naturally and accurately. That's what we mean by "being self-conscious" about how we're performing.

This doesn't mean never thinking about mechanics or specific movements. Conscious intention is involved in the learning process. We direct our awareness to particular aspects of the golf swing. We consciously evaluate the extent to which our action matches our intention. However, this is done in practice, using feedback and repetition to develop "grooved" swing habits. When it comes time to make a swing on the course, the best thing we can do is trust our body (and intuitive mind) to produce what we've practiced, without thoughts about swing mechanics, without trying to consciously direct our physical movements. As we discussed earlier, the aspect of the mind that does the best job of running our body does it through images. When you play golf, do your best to have a clear, vivid, and precise image of where you want the ball to go, and trust your body to send it there.

Often a "toss the ball" demonstration can show students how accurate they can be when they don't try too hard. I leave golf balls near a few of the chairs in the front row, then ask someone to toss me a ball. It usually lands right in my hand. I ask, "How did you do that?" Of course, the student wasn't thinking "how" to toss me the ball. The person usually says, "I just did it." I ask, "Didn't you think about how far to take your arm back to make it go the right distance, or when to release it, or how much wrist action to use?" Everyone laughs, because no one would do that to toss a ball. The point is that there were no thoughts of mechanics, but the execution was perfectly accurate, and not too hard or too soft. Perfect line and perfect feel for distance, *without trying to make sure it came out right.*

This doesn't mean that you could hit a five-iron to a spot on a green if you just don't think about how to do it. You have to have a swing motion that can physically send a ball on the line you intend, and your body has to repeat that motion until it becomes a habit. However, once you groove that movement, your body can execute it in a very precise way without conscious direction.

Many years ago in Japan, an artist was doing a brush painting that some patrons had requested. A Zen master who was an expert at this art was visiting the area, so the artist eagerly asked him to come by and watch him execute his strokes.

When asked his opinion of the painting, the Zen master said, "To be honest with you, it's rather mediocre." The artist took another piece of paper and made his brush strokes even more carefully. "What about that one?" he asked. "Sorry, but it's not even as good as the first." Again and again the artist tried harder, being ever more careful to make the right strokes. To his dismay, the master's comments were growing more discouraging.

Finally, the master said, "Excuse me, I need to step outside for a bit of fresh air before we continue." When he had gone out-

*side, the artist was delighted to have the chance to do a paint-
ing without the self-conscious feeling he had from the master
looking over his shoulder. He went right at it without thinking
about it so that he could finish before the master returned.*

*As he made his last stroke, the master came in and said,
"Perfection."*

in golf we trust

Trust is one of the most important qualities in the game of
golf. With trust, it feels like you and your golf club are
partners dancing as one. Without trust, it feels like you and
your golf club are on opposite sides in a tug-of-war.

Golfers often have a mistaken notion of trust. They think
that trusting their swing means it should be perfectly reliable.
We're human beings, not robots, so our swing doesn't repeat
exactly. What we can trust is that it will be like our signature:
following a regular and recognizable path, *as long as it isn't
interfered with.*

Unfortunately, we tend to remember poor shots much
more than good ones, and we get a distorted perspective. The
fear of hitting a bad shot undermines our confidence and interferes with swinging freely. We lose trust in our ability to
swing the golf club and produce the results we desire.

A highly regarded golf instructor asked me to work with

one of his students, an LPGA Tour golfer who was struggling with her iron play. He told me another instructor had told her to get out there and keep on hitting balls and trying to play through the trouble. "Isn't that just beating your head against a brick wall?" he asked.

"Yes, it is, if she just keeps doing the same thing as before. That approach matches Einstein's definition of insanity: doing the same thing over and over again in the same way, hoping to get a different result. On the other hand, if she approached her practice and her playing with a different attitude, then continued to go out there and play, that would be training toward something new and not a waste of time and effort." That answer satisfied him.

Then he said, "I read all about confidence and trusting your swing, but how do I tell that to a golfer who's made a whole bunch of terrible swings?" I explained that those terrible swings were a result of not trusting her basic swing, the one that gave her so much success. Her true swing was still just fine, and she still had it. However, her mistrust interfered with it. Those awful swings were a product of the interference that arose from fearing bad results.

In tournament play especially, the consequence of a bad result can overpower the intention to trust, and the muscles tighten up during the swing. Sometimes this can manifest as an awkward sudden movement, not unlike the yips in putting. Afraid that we'll make a poor swing and hit a horrible shot, we panic at the last instant. It's as if we're trying to swing and not swing at the same time. We end up with the bad shot we feared, and it becomes a self-fulfilling prophecy.

After discussing that perspective with the golfer, we went out to explore it in a practice round. If she could trust her body (i.e., her intuitive mind) to run the swing without interference, the awkward swings wouldn't show up as much. She needed to direct her thinking mind to turn over control to her body. Before each swing, she was to mentally say a phrase such as "It's all yours" or "Take over." She chose "Let it fly." That was the signal for the thinking mind to let go, and trust her body to swing the club without interference. When she did that, the swing she had trained over the years reappeared, as accurate and powerful as ever.

can you put a cat in a box?

If you try to put a cat into an open box in a corner of a room, it will hiss and scratch and fight you all the way. When you get it into the box, it will do its best to jump right out. It will fight and escape time after time. However, if you just leave the cat alone in the room, it will explore the room for a bit, and before too long it will probably climb into the box and settle there.

In the same way, if you try to suppress fears and doubts,

they will fight their way back to the surface, possibly in the middle of your backswing. However, if you take a bigger perspective, letting them come and go, they don't hold such power over you.

Some psychologists use the "Stop!" technique. If you were caught up in a thought and someone were to sneak up behind you and yell "Stop!" in your ear, it would certainly stop your train of thought. Proponents of this technique suggest that mentally yelling "Stop!" to yourself can cut the thoughts of fear or doubt.

I don't favor this approach. Although it may work in the short run, the impetus for the thoughts will still be there. Instead, you can take a bigger view. Let the thoughts come and go, and eventually, like the cat, they will settle by themselves. With practice, you can experience your thoughts without being so caught up in them.

If you stir a glass full of muddy water, the water will stay muddy. But if you remove the spoon, the dirt will settle to the bottom and the water will be clear. Similarly, struggling with your thoughts just keeps them stirred up. Instead, stop giving them energy by letting them come and go in a spacious mind of nonjudgmental awareness. After a while they will settle themselves and your mind will be clear.

to care or not to care

*I*n ancient Tibet, three beggars were talking. One said, "I wish I were the governor. He's the richest man in the town. Then I could live in comfort, and everyone would respect me." The second beggar said, "I wouldn't be content with that. I wish I were the king. He's the richest man in the country. Then I would live in luxury, and everyone would bow to me." The third beggar said, "Well, if we're going to wish, let's go all the way. I wish I were Milarepa." The other beggars were puzzled, and asked who Milarepa was.

"He's the Buddhist meditation master who lives in those mountains. He has tamed his mind, so he is always comfortable. He knows his own nature, so he doesn't need confirmation from others. He is completely content with whatever he has, so he never needs anything. That makes him the richest man in the world."

If you don't need anything, you can appreciate everything. If you have a sense of humor about how things go, the universe loves to dance with you. The more desperately you need things to come out the way you want them to, the more obstacles arise in the way of your efforts.

In golf, if you try too hard to make things come out a

particular way (like steering a shot), it usually doesn't work. If you trust the process you're doing to produce the results you intend, good results are more likely to appear. There's a big difference between confident aspiration and unconfident desperation.

People often take "not being concerned about results" to mean that they'll play best if they don't care about how the shot turns out. Some tour pros say that they putt the best when they don't care if they miss. I feel that the word "care" here can be misunderstood and become problematic. Care can mean either "have an interest in" or "worry about." I'm sure a professional golfer means he doesn't *worry* about whether or not he misses. If he had no interest in whether the ball went in the hole, he wouldn't be playing golf. And when it will make a difference of several thousand dollars in his bank account, it's hard to believe he wouldn't be interested. The nonworrying type of care means focusing on executing his routine, setting up and flowing into the stroke without a moment of hesitation.

When golfers confuse the two meanings, they try to act *as if* they don't care. Pretending that they couldn't care less makes them truly careless—they get loose and sloppy. And they know in their hearts that they *do* care, so it feels terrible. Let's get it straight—if you didn't care you wouldn't be playing golf. But you can care without worrying. If you care in the sense of being *interested,* you'll be focused and go through your process and trust your routine, and the stroke will be smooth and free. If you care as in being *worried,* you'll be unsynchronized and untrusting, and your stroke will be hesitant and bound up. Take your pick.

Dave, an instructor at a golf school, asked me for advice about his own game. He wanted to know how to "putt without caring." He said, "How do I not care? I try to feel that way, but I just can't convince myself that I don't care. I *do* care. Otherwise I wouldn't be out there playing golf." I told him the problem was with the word "care." Of course you care about making the putt. The point is not to *worry* about whether you will make it or not. I said, "Dave, this will help you get a feel for the difference between the two, and how it will affect your putting. I'm going to say two sentences to you. Pay close attention to how each one makes you feel."

"Dave, I care about you."

"Dave, I worry about you."

how to make every putt

I'd like to suggest a new definition for "making a putt." To most golfers, whether or not they make a putt is defined by whether or not it goes in the hole. This emphasizes the result of the putt more than it does the process of putting, and that interferes with the stroke. When we can be totally involved in the process and not preoccupied with the result, body and mind are synchronized. Therefore, we should have a definition of making a putt that reflects the *process* of putting more than the result of the putt.

Once Peter Jacobsen, a PGA Tour veteran, was asked how he felt about missing a putt on the last hole of a tournament. He said, "I didn't miss the putt. I made the putt. The ball missed the hole." That's exactly the point: Let's recognize the difference between *making* a putt and *holing* a putt.

To develop our new definition, let's look at the components of the *process* of putting:

1. Choosing the best line for the putt that we can
2. Getting the best feel for the pace that we can
3. Making the best stroke we can

This is all we can do; after the ball is on its way, the result is beyond our control.

Therefore, the best definition to use is this: If you rolled the ball on the line you chose, at the pace you wanted, with what you felt was a good stroke, then you *made* the putt. You may not *hole* every putt, but you can *make* every putt.

This has a powerful effect on your confidence in putting. Even the best golfers misread their share of putts. If you misread a putt, you can still walk off a green feeling that you made the putt you intended. That maintains a positive mind-set. Feeling that you missed one you "should have made" sets a negative, self-critical tone. After a round, reviewing how often your putts missed the hole isn't exactly a confidence builder. However, finishing a round with the feeling that you "made" almost all your putts leaves you feeling great about yourself as a putter. And confidence makes all the difference in the world when it comes to putting.

Brian considered himself a great ball-striker but only a fair putter. We worked on his putting before a tournament he was playing in. Standing on the practice green, I set a ball six feet from a hole and said, "The only way you can be sure of the ball going in the hole is to pick it up with your hand and place it there. And that's against the rules of golf. So what *can* you do?

"One thing is to pick the best line that you can. Another thing is to get the best feel that you can for the pace that will send it on that line to the hole. The third thing you can do is to make as good a stroke as you can, to start the ball rolling on the line you picked at the pace you want. At that point, your job is done. After that, it's between the ball, the grass, and the hole as to whether or not it goes in. All you can do is root for it."

The language we use is very important. If I had said the perfect line* and the perfect pace, there would be many ways to go wrong. By saying "the best you can" for both, you can't go wrong. That reinforces the new definition for making the putt as distinguished from holing the putt.

Brian executed a few putts focusing on this process and

---

* You can't pick the "perfect" line, because you don't know what that is until after you putt. I prefer using the word "path," in that it is a more spacious image than "line." "Path" seems to resonate more with intuitive mind, while "line" tends to evoke analytical mind.

using the new definition. He stroked the ball very well, "made" almost all the putts, and "holed" many of them. I said, "Actually, Brian, you were already a great putter. There was just a lot of baggage—expectations, trying, and worrying—that got in the way. You were *trying* to make putts and thinking about *how* to putt. With this simpler approach, the baggage is gone and you can just step up and putt."

Two months later at the finals of Qualifying School, in six rounds of high-pressure golf, Brian had thirty-three birdies and an eagle, no three-putts, and holed every putt inside six feet.

putt with imagination

The best preparation for any shot is to have an image that is as complete and precise as possible. For your putts, imagine the ball rolling the full distance to the hole. See in your mind's eye the way it will change speed and direction. See the path it will take all the way to the exact point on the edge of the hole where the ball will fall in. In the following pages are techniques, exercises, and routines that will help you feel confident over any putt.

Read for Speed

Reading a putt on a sloping green, you might ask your caddie or your playing partner, "How much do you think it will break?" It may surprise you, but whatever they answer will be wrong. The only correct response they can make is, "It all depends on how firmly you're going to stroke it." How much a putt breaks depends completely on how fast it's rolling. The faster the ball is traveling, the less effect gravity will have on it, and therefore the less it will break.

How do you choose whether to stroke a putt gently and play for the maximum break, or to stroke it firmly and play for the minimum break? A good way to decide is by considering the risk factor. The more severe the slope, the more you should choose to play for maximum break. This reduces the risk of going too far past the hole. On a less severe slope (and especially if the putt is uphill), you can make a firmer stroke and play for less break. This reduces the risk of spike marks, grain, or uneven spots in the green deflecting the putt as it slows down.

Your planning process starts long before you get to your ball. As you approach the green, get a sense of its overall slope by surveying the surrounding terrain and determining the high and low areas of the green. Remember, greens tend to slope away from nearby mountains and toward nearby water (like a lake, a creek, or even the ocean). For some types of greens, the grain of the grass is also a factor to be taken into account. Then decide on the pace you want the putt to roll.

Read the Putt Backward

The best way to read a putt is to start at the hole. Examine the area around the hole. See the direction from which a ball would roll most easily into the hole, and the exact spot on the edge it will cross. That point becomes the *effective center* of the hole for your putt.

Then work backward from there to your ball, imagining the path and pace your ball will need to travel to enter the hole at the spot you picked. (Keep in mind that it will be going fastest at the start, so it will break least at the beginning and most at the end of the putt.) You may be surprised to discover how much break you're planning to play. Most golfers play for far less break than they need to, which is why most putts are missed below the hole.

Images for Putting

To keep your target in mind, imagine that the hole is a clock-face, with 6:00 toward your ball. Pick the "time" on the clock rim where you expect the ball to enter the hole. For example, you may see a right-to-left breaking putt entering the hole at 4:30, or a left-to-right putt with just a bit of break entering at 7:00. That time on the clock is your effective center of the hole.

To help you stroke your putt with the correct speed, keep in your mind an image of how the ball will enter the hole. Thinking to yourself about how hard to swing the club while putting is a surefire recipe for disaster. Nearly every golfer has thought, "Make sure you get it to the hole," and then sent the ball six feet past it. The thought "It's downhill, so go easy on it" usually results in a tentative, decelerating stroke that leaves the ball well short of the hole. Instead, use your imagination. On an uphill putt, imagine the ball diving into the hole, striking the middle of the back wall. This gives your body the message to stroke the ball firmly, without you needing to think, "Hit it hard." On a downhill putt, imagine the ball just trickling over the front edge. This gives your body the message to stroke the ball gently, but without the hesitation that comes from the fear of the ball going far past the hole.

When you putt with imagination, you'll be pleasantly surprised at how many putts pour into the hole exactly the way you imagined.

Long Lag Putts

One of the most common approaches to long putts is to lag, meaning to try to roll the ball near the hole without really trying to get it in.

The most common technique that is applied to this approach is to imagine a circle, six feet in diameter, around the hole. If you're inside this, you have no more than three feet remaining for your second putt. The purpose of this approach is to take the pressure off the long putts. Feeling the pressure to get close enough for a tap-in, we try too hard, causing us to either tense up and leave it short or be too aggressive and knock the ball far past the hole. Having a big circle as a target is supposed to help us relax and not try too hard.

However, there are also problems with this technique. One is that a circle two yards wide is too big a target, not specific enough for the mind to give the body a precise image of what is supposed to happen. The more precise the image one has in mind, the better chance there is that the body will produce it. Too vague a target causes a lack of focus in executing the shot.

Another problem with "lagging" to a circle around the hole occurs if we miss the circle. Then we think, "I must really be bad. I can't even get the ball inside a six-foot-wide circle." This can be very discouraging and make us worry about making the next one to avoid a three-putt.

I recommend picturing the putt actually going in the hole, over a spot on the edge, even on long putts. Make the best read you can and simply give the ball the best roll you can. The more specific your target is, the better results you'll get.

Then there's the issue of distance. Distance is a more critical factor than direction in making or missing long putts, so it's important to gauge the distance as well as we can. For uphill and downhill putts, some instructors recommend that the golfer imagine a hole in a different spot than the actual hole, on the line of the putt, but in front of the real hole for downhill putts and behind the real hole for uphill putts. The steeper the grade, the farther away one pictures the imaginary "target" hole. The problem with this approach is that you're sending mixed signals to your body, giving it two targets to deal with. Although you're trying to hit the ball as far as the imaginary hole, it's hard to block out the actual hole that is your real target. This conflicting information means body and mind aren't synchronized.

Instead, focus on an image of the pace at which the putt will enter the actual hole. It will make you more precise about reading the green and getting a feel for the distance. As for the pace of the putt, the image you give your body of how the ball will enter the hole directs how firmly the putt is struck. As discussed before, for uphill putts, imagine that it will dive in and hit against the back of the cup. For level putts, picture it pouring into the hole. For downhill putts, picture it just trickling over the front edge.

A 6-handicap golfer came to me wanting to know how to be less hesitant on downhill putts. We talked about the approach outlined here. Seeing them just trickling over the edge took away the fear of them rolling far beyond the hole, so it freed him up to make a smoother stroke, rolling the ball all the way there. His next round he only needed twenty-five putts.

Exercises for Putting with Imagination

Guessing Game for Developing Feel

The key to getting the distance right on long putts is getting a good feel for the speed of the green. Here's a putting drill that will quickly give you a feel for the pace of the green.

On a level area of the practice green, line up several balls about twenty feet away from the fringe. Set up to the first ball and focus on the distance from the ball to the fringe. Then make your regular stroke, putting toward the fringe. *Keep your head looking down after the putt is struck.* Guess whether it will be "short," "long," or "just right" at the edge of the fringe *before you look up.* Then look up to watch where the ball stops compared to your guess. Repeat the process with each ball.

In this exercise, the sense of touch is separated from the sense of sight. That's why it's important that you make your guess based on feel before you look up. Then watching the ball come to a stop creates a feedback loop that promotes rapid learning, so your feel for the pace of the green develops quickly. You'll be surprised at how few balls it takes before your guesses become accurate and the putts start finishing right at the edge.

Two additional benefits result from this drill. First, you practice keeping your head still through the stroke, which is an important fundamental for good putting. Second, since you're not directing the ball toward a hole, your stroke will become smoother and more consistent. Ben Crenshaw has said that his putting stroke is the smoothest when he's not putting at a hole.

Practice this drill for uphill and downhill putts as well, and if you have time, do it for longer distances. When you're facing a long putt on the course, you'll be able to address it with confidence in your feel for the speed of the green.

Leapfrog Game for Developing Touch

Most champion golfers excel in putting and the short game. They are usually described as having "a great touch around the greens." Here's a game for developing touch.

Take three tees to a level area of the putting green. Stick one tee in the ground, then take two paces and put a second tee in the green, then three more paces and insert the last tee. The first putt starts at the first tee and is supposed to go just past the second tee.

Your goal is to fit as many balls as you can in the space between the second tee and the farthest tee, with each successive ball going past ("leapfrogging") the previous one. For each successful "leapfrog," you score a point. If a putt doesn't make it past the previous ball, you lose a point, and you still need to go past that ball on your next putt. Once a ball rolls past the far tee, your turn is over. Your final score is the number of points on the last ball before the far tee. You can play this game uphill and downhill (that's the hardest) as well. Play alone and see if you can beat your own best score; play against a friend to develop touch under the pressure of competition.

Once you've mastered this (10 points or more in the space of three paces), set the second tee three paces away (still leaving three paces to fit balls into). Finally, do the drill setting the second tee five paces away. Score a 10 that way and you have the touch of a pro.

Warm-up Routine
on the Putting Green

Here's a pre-round putting warm-up routine I have given tour players and amateurs alike.

Step 1: Putt to Nowhere. In an open area of the practice green, stroke a few putts with no target at all. Vary the distances you roll the putts. Do this until you feel your stroke is smooth and consistent.

Step 2: Putt to the Fringe. Do the Guessing Game for Developing Feel described earlier.

Step 3: Long Putts. Stroke several long putts (ranging from twenty-five to forty feet) toward various holes on the practice green. If you hole one, don't putt the same putt again.

Step 4. (Note: This part of the routine is only done on a course with very undulating greens, and a practice green that has similar slopes and speed.) After the long putts, roll a few fifteen-footers with big breaks, to get a feel for the relationship of pace to break. Experiment with a variety of lines and speeds for each putt. If you hole one, don't putt the same putt again.

Step 5: Short Putts. Stroke several two-foot putts, focusing primarily on keeping your head steady and listening for the putt going into the hole. See it go in only in your peripheral vision. These very short putts reinforce confidence with that "feel good" sound of the ball rattling into the bottom of the cup again and again without a miss, and it is a virtually identical stroke to the one you'll use for putts of four or five feet. Now you're ready for the golf course.

You might ask, "Why didn't you include in the warm-up some practice on the eight-foot putts that we feel we should make during the round?" First, it needs to be pointed out that getting a feel for distance isn't much of an issue for these putts, especially having already done the "feel" drill. Second, there's a sharply increasing likelihood of missing putts as their length increases beyond a few feet. When you miss a putt that you think you "should" hole, even in practice, it undermines your confidence. Why practice missing putts?

don't count your money

For the best execution of a golf shot, body and mind need to be synchronized, which can only happen in the present. That applies not only to a single golf shot but also to a hole, a round, and a tournament.

Being in the present means focusing only on the shot at hand. If you add anything to the situation, such as the meaning of a putt for your score, your mind leaves the present and gets out of sync with your body. "This is for birdie. If I make it, that would give me a chance to shoot my best round ever. If I miss, that would be another blown opportunity." When you think this way, you're already handing in your scorecard, and you haven't even putted yet. As Kenny Rogers sings in "The Gambler," "Don't count your money while you're sittin' at the table. . . ."

Instead, relate to what is actually going on in the present. A putt is a ball, a few feet of grass, and a hole. That's all that exists in the present. Any meaning you add to it has to do with the past (e.g., to make up for that last bogey and get back to even par) or the future (e.g., to put me into a tie for the lead and give me a chance to win).

When a round is going well and then turns sour, thoughts of past or future are usually the culprit. You may take a seemingly easy hole for granted and start worrying about a difficult one coming up later. Then you get angry at yourself for messing up the so-called easy hole, so you keep telling yourself what you "should" have done on that past hole for the next couple of holes and mess them up, too. Not a pretty picture, albeit a familiar one.

If you get off to a bad start or are falling behind, projecting into the future can make you lose patience and get out of your game plan. You might try risky shots thinking you need to "make something happen," and all that you make happen is the end to your chance of winning. You never know what the other player will do.

Assuming that her opponent has the advantage, a golfer will often give up on a hole or try something desperate. When she's in the trees and her opponent is in the fairway, instead of safely playing out she goes for broke (which is how she usually ends up). But there's no guarantee that the other player will hit a good approach shot. If you play the smartest shot you can and keep yourself in the game, you still have a chance. If you beat yourself, your opponent doesn't even have to play well to win.

The reverse assumption, that you've "got it in the bag," can be even more dangerous. In football or basketball, leading teams get in trouble when they start to play a "prevent defense" too early in the game. If the other team catches up, the first team has a hard time rousing the energy to go on the offensive again. In the same way, if you think you've got the match or the tournament won, that image of the future gives a message to your body that you're finished. All your systems start to shift into low gear, as if the next thing you're going to do is sit down in the clubhouse and have a drink. You stand up on the tee and it's as if your body is saying, "What are we doing here? We're supposed to be in the bar." It's hard to get started up again and focus on the shots you still have to play.

A Sudden Turn of Events

Here's another example of how predicting the future on the golf course can get us into a lot of trouble.

In the last round of a professional tournament, Alex and two other golfers were tied for the lead. They played together in the last group. On the first hole, a par-5, all three put their drives in the fairway. For their second shots, Alex laid up just in front of the green, but the other two pulled their approaches deep into the trees and bushes to the left. His fellow competitors both found their balls, but in very bad spots. Alex pitched on, finishing just eight feet below the hole. One of the other players managed to get his ball onto the green, but it finished about twenty-five feet from the hole. The other had a more difficult shot, over bushes and between trees, with a downhill roll to the pin. The ball flew up, bounced twice, rolled onto the green, curled around, and went into the hole for an eagle. Then the golfer who was twenty-five feet away lined up his putt, stroked it, and in it went for a birdie. Being on the green with a short putt and his opponents in trouble, Alex assumed he would be at least 1 and possibly 2 up on the others. Now he had to make birdie just to keep from being 2 down. When he missed, it frustrated him and he missed a similar putt on the next hole as well.

When we assume things will turn out a particular way, we set ourselves up for the shock of the unexpected. Especially difficult is a change of fortunes that shifts one's position from a seeming advantage to a disadvantage. This can be disconcerting. Expectations are shattered, and a low-pressure shot suddenly becomes a high-pressure one. The contrast makes the tension feel even worse, creating a torrent of distracting mental activity, ruining one's composure. The chance of making a relaxed, confident stroke is practically gone.

Instead, take an attitude that prevents the shock. When you're in an advantageous position, expect that your opponents are going to hole their shots. That way, you'll never be surprised when they do.

It's important to keep your focus as much as possible on your own game. Then what your opponents are doing won't influence you as much. The best frame of mind is to regard the other players as "fellow competitors," which is the official language of the rules of golf. In fact, you *are* fellow competitors, because you are all in competition against your common opponent: the golf course.

In golf we don't compete directly against the other player. No one is throwing the ball in a way that makes it harder for you to hit. No one is trying to block your shot. No one is swinging at you. In golf we compare scores after the hole (match play) or the round (stroke play). The winner is the one who had the best score *against the golf course.* If you compete against the course rather than your opponents, you're less likely to defeat yourself through assumptions, predictions, and other mental mistakes.

Keep your thinking in the present—don't count your chickens before they hatch, and you won't be so disappointed with a broken egg once in a while.

the slow-motion walk-up

Hasten slowly and you will soon arrive.

—Milarepa, eleventh-century
Tibetan Buddhist master

Chris, a good junior golfer, came for a lesson. He complained that his swing gave him trouble when he "got quick at the top." That usually refers to an especially quick start to the downswing. It sometimes reflects a premature transition, starting the downswing before the backswing is complete. He showed me his swing routine, how he approached and set up to the ball, then how he swung. He fairly charged up to address the ball. I asked about his pace of play on the course. He said, "Fast. I can't wait to get to the ball and hit it."

I asked him to go through his routine, not trying to alter his swing in any way, but this time to approach the ball in slow motion. He looked puzzled but did as requested. To his amazement, his quickness at the top was gone.

His youthful eagerness to play every shot meant that his tempo began to increase, little by little, without him noticing it. It's like driving a car and finding to your surprise that you are going much faster than the speed limit. Your speed had increased in tiny increments, so small that you didn't notice them.* With each one, you had become accustomed to the speed and therefore hadn't noticed the next small increase. Eventually, you realized how fast you were going.

When you slowed down, in contrast to the higher speed you'd gotten used to, your original speed seemed very slow. When you were used to going eighty miles an hour, slowing down to sixty felt as if you were doing forty.

Although Chris was going quickly through his routine (and consequently through the transition at the top of his swing), it didn't feel particularly fast because he had gotten used to it. When he approached the ball in slow motion, it set a slower tempo for the whole swing. In fact, it was his normal tempo, so what appeared was his normal swing.

The "Slow-Motion Walk-Up" works for players at all levels, and it even has an impact on tour players and other top-level golfers. Tempo and timing are so refined for these players that the slightest variation can make a huge difference in their results. At PGA Tour Qualifying School one year, Anthony, a college All-American and former PGA Tour player, was having lunch with another player and me. He excused himself, saying he needed to get to the range and work on his swing. He said he was getting quick at the top. I asked if he'd

---

* In psychology, increments of perception are called JND's, for "Just Noticeable Differences." When a change in the environment or one's behavior happens that is smaller than a JND, it isn't noticed, but the body acclimates to it and it becomes what feels normal.

like to try something that wasn't involved with changing his swing technique, and told him to do the slow-motion walk-up, without trying to "fix" his swing in any way.

The next day he approached the ball as if he were stealth-ily stalking it and hit brilliant shots. He posted the low score of the day and said, "Doc, if there was ever a day that I thought I could shoot 59, this was it."

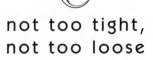

not too tight, not too loose

A musician came for instruction from the Buddha in prac-ticing meditation. He asked, "How should I hold my mind when I practice? Should I try to concentrate hard and keep it under tight control, or should I relax and let it wander wher-ever it wants to go?"

The Buddha answered the musician with a question. "When you tune your instrument, do you make the strings too tight or too loose?"

The musician replied, "Neither too tight nor too loose. I make them just so."

The Buddha said, "In the same way as you tune the strings of your instrument, so you should hold your mind in medita-tion. Not too tight, not too loose, just so."

This story is one of the oldest in the Buddhist tradition. It comes from a collection of instructions on meditation given by the Buddha, each in response to a question from a student. It applies to many aspects of golf and life. For example, if we grip the club too tightly (the white-knuckle approach), we lose feel and the capability of letting our wrists and hands release fully. If our grip is too loose, the club can turn in our hands and the swing can feel floppy. If we try too hard, get too uptight, it interferes with swinging freely. If we relax too much, we don't focus on the shot and our swing becomes sloppy.

Modern sports psychology validates the principal of "not too tight, not too loose" in its analysis of the relationship between performance and emotional intensity. When there is little emotional intensity, the level of performance is very low. This reflects not caring at all, so no effort or energy goes into performance. That is the quality of "too loose." As emotional intensity increases, so does the level of performance. Peak performance is reached at a medium level of intensity—not too high, not too low. Performance deteriorates as emotional intensity increases beyond that optimal level. When there is high emotional intensity, the level of performance is again, very low. This means that when we are extremely emotional, we are extremely ineffective. That is the quality of "too tight."

"Just so" is that level of emotional intensity at which peak performance is attained. Everyone's "just so" level is a bit different, in the same way that the ideal tension for different strings on an instrument would be different. Just as the musician couldn't describe the tautness his string needed in order to be in tune, no one can tell you an exact formula for your ideal amount of emotional intensity. You have to feel it, intuitively, for yourself. You won't be able to describe what it is, but you can describe what it is not—it's not too tight and not too loose.

beware of trying for a few extra yards

All too often we try to get something extra out of our drives, and the results are usually the opposite of what we desire. Even if we're lucky enough to find the ball, it has traveled less than our usual distance.

The golf swing is a series of muscle movements, all in sequence. Any interference with that sequence, such as extra muscle tension, interrupts the flow of the swing, causing errors in body action, swing path, and contact point. The average golfer's idea of "trying to hit it farther" actually causes an excess tightening of muscles, which shortens the arc of the swing and reduces the whipping action of the arms, resulting in a *loss* of distance. That's why Bobby Jones said, "Trying for a few extra yards at the last moment is the cause of most of the mistakes that happen on the tee."

Don't Let Your Ego Betray You

Most average players try to hit every shot as far as they possibly can. Ego is the culprit here: We think that how far we can hit a particular club is the measure of how good we are. But that's not the point of the game of golf. Accuracy and consistency are much more important for lower golf scores.

Tour players swing at only 80 percent of their maximum power on most shots. It's called playing within yourself, and the purpose is to make a consistent, smooth swing that produces consistent distances for each club.

Average golfers almost always leave their approach shots far short of the hole. Again, ego is at fault: We choose the club that would reach the hole only if we hit it absolutely perfectly. This creates a subconscious tendency to try to "kill the ball," which causes all kinds of problems. With this attitude, a perfect shot is unlikely, which is why we very rarely reach our target. Instead, when faced with an approach to a green, choose the club that will take you near the back of the green with a perfect shot. More often than not, you'll end up about in the middle, not too far from the hole.

Every Drive Is a Layup

Most golfers get excellent results from a layup shot. All we're trying to do is put the ball in position for the next shot. We're not trying to hit it as far as we can or trying to get it close to the hole. Usually it's not aimed near a hazard (in fact, we're often playing it to avoid a hazard). For these reasons it's a low-pressure shot, so quite often we make a very smooth, relaxed, rhythmic swing. And quite often our best shots are produced.

One time a student complained to me that he had been hitting his driver very poorly, so he tried using his three-wood off the tee, since he always hit it well. But now he was starting to hit his three-wood as badly as his driver. He had the "trying for a few extra yards" problem. He was always trying to hit the tee shot as far as he possibly could, no matter what club he had in his hands. At the start of our playing lesson that afternoon, I suggested that he think of the tee shot as a layup shot, picking a spot on the fairway that he was confident he could reach with his three-wood. He was delighted as his relaxed swing sent the ball flying to and beyond the spot he picked, right down the middle.

Try thinking of every tee shot on a par-4 or par-5 hole as a layup shot. No matter what club you use, instead of just trying to hit it as far as you can, pick a spot on the fairway that's well within reach. This reduces the tendency to swing too hard and gives you a much better chance of hitting a good shot. You'll be surprised how many times that relaxed swing sends the ball even farther down the fairway than you could imagine.

nothing special,
nothing extra

Brian had entered the Qualifying School for the PGA Tour for twelve years, but had fallen short every time. The Q-School is actually a series of tournaments, culminating in the finals, a grueling six-round tournament. It is the ultimate pressure cooker, as each golfer's career for the next year is on the line.

I met Brian two months before the Q-School finals. He told me about his career in golf, his hopes and fears, his strengths and weaknesses. We talked about how to prepare for a shot and how to respond to results, both good and bad. We discussed how he and other golfers sometimes sabotage themselves when things are going well, how fear of bad results prevents making a free swing. He started to have a new perspective toward the game and how he treated himself on the golf course. In those two months, we distinguished key issues that would impact the quality of his play. They were:

- Staying in the present and not being distracted by thoughts of outcome (score or standing), neither his own nor his opponents'.
- Establishing composure and focus. This meant feeling

settled and having a clear image in mind of the shot he wanted to produce before addressing the ball.

- Trusting his swing and shot-making ability, and staying free from the self-sabotaging tendency of expecting to mess up after things are going well for a while.
- Not being so hard on himself when he makes a mistake, and managing strong feelings like anger, excitement, and frustration.

We established goals for the tournament. However, unlike the usual result-oriented goals involving scores or standings, we chose process goals that related to the keys we were working on: to have good images for every shot, to stay in the present for every shot, to be committed and ready for every shot. The most important point was, "Take care of the process and the results will take care of themselves."

On the cover of the yardage book that he consults before each shot, Brian wrote the following phrases to remind him of his keys:

For staying in the present, he wrote: *One Round at a Time, One Hole at a Time, One Shot at a Time.*

For composure and focus, he wrote: *Gather Yourself—Good Picture.*

For trusting himself and playing within himself, he wrote: *Nothing Special, Nothing Extra.*

Brian applied these so well that for most of the tournament he was totally in the zone. He posted a total of 30 under par, finishing second in a field of 170 golfers, many of whom were PGA Tour veterans. It was the best golf Brian had ever played in a professional tournament, and he'd done it in the toughest tournament there is.

RESPONSE TO RESULTS

Response to results is the third stage of the PAR Approach. The best responses to results are those that reinforce successes and help you learn from mistakes without getting down on yourself. This section includes a unique "post-shot routine" and ways to recognize and undo negativity and self-sabotage, as well as a simple yet powerful technique for changing habits. If you reinforce good shots with positive feelings and self-encouragement, have a minimum of emotional distress around poor shots, maintain a sense of humor, and refrain from beating yourself up, those ways of responding to results will give you the best chance of success.

the post-shot routine

Golfers need to reinforce positive experiences and learn from negative ones. There are reactions to good and bad shots that are common to most golfers. If we hit a drive down the middle of the fairway, we might bend down and pick up our tee before the shot has even landed. If we hit a poor shot, we follow it to the finish and get upset.

Here's a post-shot routine that reverses those responses. When you hit a shot that comes out just the way you pictured it, get some emotion going. Give yourself a silent "Yes!" or some other expression of positive emotion. That reinforces the experience. Hold your finish and follow the flight of the ball until it stops. That imprints the image in your mind so that you can call on it when you face a similar shot or need to make the same shot in a more challenging situation. Store it in your "video library of greatest hits."

If you hit a poor shot, instead of erupting in a storm of emotion, get somewhat detached and intellectual about it. I recommend that you say, "Hmmm. Interesting." To remove yourself from the outcome even further, you can say, "How unlike me." (That usually gets a pretty good laugh when I suggest it at golf schools.) You'll probably have an initial reaction of anger or frustration, but it's important to clear the emotional response as soon as possible, because emotions cloud awareness. If you're emotional, you won't be able to tell what just happened. Insight does not appear in the midst of emotional upheaval. If you keep your cool, you can reflect on what you just experienced and learn from it.

When a shot is hit poorly, most people (after they've calmed down and stopped moaning) try to figure out what they did wrong. It is extremely important at this point in the post-shot routine that you *do not try to fix your swing.* Yes, the unsatisfactory shot was a result of the swing you made. However, something produced that version of your swing. You didn't forget how to swing since your last shot. Something got in the way. Take a step back and think about what it was that interfered with your swing. Reflect on your preparation and state of mind. Did you have a good picture? Were you committed to the club and shot selection? Were you composed, settled, and ready when you started the swing?

Did you have mechanically oriented thoughts during the swing? Did you trust the swing or try to consciously steer or guide the shot? Did you do an anyway?

If, on reflection, you felt properly prepared mentally, review your alignment, ball position, or other aspects of your physical setup.

If any of these were the culprit, then there's no need to question or try to fix your swing. Just do your best to set-up properly next time.

Remember, whatever faults there are in a swing, it doesn't

generally work to try to fix them on the course. When we work on our swing during a round, we usually create a tangle of compensating movements that makes us feel tied in knots. So even if you think it's broken, don't fix it.

Because of "poverty mentality," we take a good deal of convincing to believe the best about ourselves, but readily accept the worst. For example, it takes holing a lot of putts over many rounds before we begin to think of ourselves as good putters. But when we start missing putts, all too quickly we begin to think of ourselves as bad putters. Often we relate to one errant shot as a sign that something is wrong with our swing, and we spend the whole rest of the round struggling to fix it. With the perspective of unconditional confidence, one bad shot won't lead us to doubt ourselves.

thanks for the memories

Why do negative memories and thoughts predominate in our experience? As we grew up, good behavior was expected and bad was punished. We treat ourselves that way on the course, expecting perfection and punishing any mistakes. No wonder it can be hard to relax and enjoy ourselves.

Emotional experiences register more strongly in memory than ordinary experiences. They get a special "tag" because of the emotional charge associated with them. We're hardwired that way, a survival mechanism inherited from prehistoric times.

If a cavewoman walked around a big boulder and came upon a den of saber-toothed tigers, it would be helpful for her survival to remember that boulder. The same goes for a powerful positive emotion, as when she walked around another boulder and discovered a grove of trees full of delicious fruit. But if she walked around a big rock and just found more rocks on the other side, there would be no reason to waste precious cranial capacity remembering that big rock.

In the same way, if I asked you what you had for breakfast two years ago today, you probably wouldn't remember. But if on that day your wife had told you she was expecting your first child, you'd remember the moment vividly. The same amount of time has gone by, but one experience was charged with far more emotion.

When we make a four-foot putt, there may be some relief but not usually a lot of emotion. However, when we miss a four-foot putt, there is often a reaction of frustration or anger. That emotional reaction imprints more strongly in our memory, which means the image of missing the putt is more likely to come to mind when we encounter a similar four-footer. That undermines our confidence and we're more likely to miss.

Soon it's a self-fulfilling prophecy and we feel like a poor putter. This cycle is one reason why senior golfers sometimes struggle with putting. It's not that their nerves are less steady; it's just that they remember more misses.

If you build up a stockpile of negative memories about a situation on the golf course (or elsewhere in your life), you will expect to mess things up when you encounter a similar situation. As we saw in "You Produce What You Fear," those expectations are likely to be fulfilled. This is why it's so important not to be consumed by negative reactions to poor shots. In your post-shot routine, do your best to replace negative emotions with detached observation. Remember, "Hmmm. Interesting."

the angry guy

*O*nce *a Zen master was listening to a student complain about his uncontrollable temper. The student said, "I'm a very angry person. Please help me to change."*

"Sounds like a big problem. Let's see this terrible anger of yours," the master demanded of the student.

"I can't show it to you. I'm not angry right now."

"Then when can you demonstrate it for me?" the master asked.

"I don't know. It takes me by surprise."

"This anger must not be your true nature. If it were, your anger would be available for display anytime. If it's not there all the time, and you can't even summon it when you want to, you are not an angry person."

This story illustrates a vitally important point. Seeing characteristics as permanent parts of ourselves makes them unworkable, unchangeable. Seeing almost everything we do as a habit or combination of habits means that there is always the possibility of change.

Let's describe the same person in two different ways. First: There goes an angry guy. Second: There goes a guy who has a habit of getting angry. Which description makes the person sound more "workable"? Almost everyone says it's the second description. When we explore why, we recognize that to say someone is an angry person is to say that anger is a permanent part of their nature.

To say that someone has a habit of getting angry doesn't imply that it's part of their nature. If it's a habit, even a very strong one, there's a possibility for change. That's why thinking about our own or others' behavior in terms of habit rather than nature makes life so much more workable.

When it comes to things we do on the golf course, whether it's during our swing, in response to our swing, or between shots, it is much more workable to regard them as changeable habits rather than permanent attributes of our game.

This idea can be particularly helpful when it comes to working with emotions on the course. We might try to suppress an emotion like anger, but that just bottles it up. Eventually, it finds a way to leak out, often at the most inopportune moment. We might feel good about getting it out of our system, acting out what we're feeling. That's the club-thrower's mentality. However, rather than eliminate the emotion, this just reinforces it and invites more eruptions.

The key is to change your attitude, not try to get rid of the emotion. Neither suppress nor indulge the emotion. Acknowledge the emotion's intensity but drop the story line connected with it. In that way, the energy of anger over a bad shot can be transformed into intensity of focus on the next shot.

how to make
a flower blossom

How do you make a flower blossom? You wouldn't pull up on the stem to make it taller. You wouldn't peel back the petals from the bud to make them open up. If you tried to force it to blossom that way, you would actually prevent it from doing so.

Instead of forcing a flower to blossom, we need to nurture it. We need to give it the right conditions: sunlight, water, soil, fertilizer. But those are just circumstances. What is it that actually makes the flower blossom?

Nothing external makes it blossom—it is its *nature* to grow and unfold. It will do so beautifully given the right nurturing conditions. A flower doesn't need to try to blossom.

We can apply this principle to ourselves in our learning

and development, in changing habits in our golf game and our life. Our nature is basic goodness, which includes the capacity for awareness and the impetus to learn and grow. Therefore, like a flower, we don't need to force ourselves to change or try extra hard to learn and grow. It's our nature to do so. All we need to do is give ourselves the right conditions. Such conditions include the fresh air of unconditional confidence, the earth of our inherent basic goodness, the water of positive attitudes and intentions, the sunlight of nonjudgmental awareness, and the fertilizer of coaching and practice. With those as our environment, our natural tendency to learn and grow will flourish.

It is also important to remember that a flower *can't* blossom if something prevents sunlight or water from reaching it. We must make sure we clear away obstacles to the optimum conditions for learning and performing in golf. Negative self-talk blocks the flow of confidence. Fear, anxiety, and self-doubt create tensions that block us from relaxing and swinging freely. Tying our self-worth to the result of a golf shot puts pressure on us. Getting caught up in emotions of anger, frustration, envy, or depression creates clouds of turmoil, blocking the sunlight of awareness.

There's an old adage, "If at first you don't succeed, try, try again." That's true if we know the appropriate way to try, which is actually more like *trusting* than trying. Unfortunately, when we try harder at golf, we usually add more tension and the uptight control of our thinking mind. It's like quicksand—the harder you try to get out, the more stuck you get. That couldn't be truer on the golf course. The harder we try to make the swing come out "right," the more self-conscious control we exert. This interferes with our tempo and flow and makes our swing even worse. The harder we try to make sure the ball goes where we want it to, the more we get caught in steering instead of swinging freely, and the more likely that the shot will go awry.

To learn and grow in our golf game or anything else, the best we can do is trust in our nature and give ourselves the optimum conditions for that nature to express itself. "Pebbles in the Bowl" presents a technique for doing just that.

pebbles in the bowl

A young monk was spending some time each day in meditation and contemplation. He wondered how many of his thoughts during those sessions were virtuous (about doing good deeds) or nonvirtuous (about deeds based on hatred, greed, or prejudice). He collected a pile of pebbles and put them in front of himself. He also placed a bowl to his left and another to his right. As he meditated, he would put a pebble in the left-hand bowl when he recognized a virtuous thought. For a nonvirtuous thought, he would put a pebble in the right-hand bowl. At the end of the first day, he looked down to see how he had done and was surprised to see that all the pebbles were in the "nonvirtu-

ous" bowl. Without judging himself, he simply continued this practice, starting over each day. After a few days, the number of pebbles in the two bowls was about equal. After a few more days, almost all the pebbles were in the "virtuous" bowl.

This story from a Buddhist text several hundred years old describes a simple yet powerful technique for changing habits. By combining intention with nonjudgmental awareness, we create the ideal supportive conditions for the flower of our learning to blossom naturally. We don't have to change our habits by trying to force ourselves to be different. That would be like peeling back the petals to make the flower blossom. If we trust that it is our nature to learn and grow, all we need to do is "put pebbles in the bowl."

Just as the monk had the intention to think virtuous thoughts, we have to establish our intentions to overcome undesirable habits. Then we need to apply nonjudgmental awareness to the habitual behavior we want to change. Intention and awareness are like the water and sunshine we give to a flower.

It is necessary that the awareness we bring to bear be nonjudgmental. Judging ourselves adds the interference of emotional energy to the situation. Such judging is an expression of "negative negativity," a term coined by my teacher, Chögyam Trungpa. We do something wrong and then beat ourselves up for doing something wrong; we feel bad about something and then we feel bad about feeling bad. Judging ourselves creates an effect that is the opposite of our intention. The emotional energy directed toward the habit actually reinforces it, making it more likely to reappear.

By directing our awareness toward the habit that we wish to change, we notice it sooner and sooner each time it arises. First we notice it after we've done it. Before long we notice it as it is happening. Then we notice it just as it starts. Eventually, we notice the impulse to engage in the habit and catch ourselves before we actually do it. Finally, even the impulse fades away.

The combination of intention and nonjudgmental awareness works to change a wide range of habits. We can change habits of our body, speech, or mind. For example, we can change the habit of leaving most of our putts short of the hole. We can change the habit of negative self-talk. We can change the habit of thinking about our score before the round is over.

Ways to Change Habits

Make a Mark

There are different ways to use intention and nonjudgmental awareness to change habits. One is simply counting, like putting pebbles in a bowl. Since pebbles and bowls are a bit awkward on the golf course, I have my players use their scorecards or yardage books. They are to write the name of the habit and make a tick mark each time they notice the behavior they want to change. (Shane, a touring professional, calls it the tick trick.) Count the marks at the end of the round and that's it for the day. Amazingly, the daily total decreases dramatically after very few rounds.

Here's an example. Russ was a former PGA Tour player who had gotten into the habit of complaining about almost every shot. His playing partners made fun of it, but they were actually getting fed up. He'd tried to stop his negative comments but couldn't seem to. The madder he got at himself for doing it, the more it seemed to happen. He definitely wanted to change. When we started working together, that habit was our first target.

I asked him to write "Complaining" in the bottom line of his scorecard and to make a mark each time he complained about a shot. I told him not to try to stop the habit, but just to mark it down each time he noticed that it happened.

The first round he had sixty complaints. The next round he had twenty-two. The next round he had seven. The fourth round he had none.

He continued to be aware of his responses to results, and noticed an unexpected effect. I had not mentioned anything about how he might react in place of complaining. However, he found himself spontaneously seeing positive possibilities instead of making complaints. He described his new response to hitting a shot in the trees, saying, "In the past, I would have just moaned, 'I'm dead.' Now I see an opening, and say to myself, 'If I pitch out of there, I'll be a nine-iron away from the hole. I can hit it close and give myself a chance to save par.' What a difference this has made in how well I play and how much I enjoy playing."

Avoiding the anyways is an example of a habit every golfer would benefit from changing. Seeing how they lead to poor results gives us the inspiration and *intention* to avoid the anyways. With that intention, whenever you play, apply *nonjudgmental awareness,* "just noticing" every time you do an anyway. On your scorecard, on the bottom line, where you would write a player's name, write the word "Anyways." Each time you realize that a shot you played was an anyway, just make a mark along that line, under the hole where it happened. It's important not to judge and criticize yourself for doing it (that's the *non*judgmental part). Just notice that it was an anyway, mark it down, and let it go.

You can support the habit-changing process by positive reinforcement as well. Give yourself a pat on the back by making a check mark for a "good catch" each time you catch yourself about to do an anyway, or other habit you intend to change.

You can use this "tick trick" method to change "yes or no" habits, those you either do or don't do. Here are some examples.

- Thinking about the future: the score, future holes you have to play, winning or losing the match or tournament, what you'll say to reporters
- Thinking about the past: repeatedly criticizing yourself for an earlier mistake; replaying past shots or rounds in your mind
- Leaving putts short or leaving approach shots short (both common habits among high handicappers)

- Negative self-talk, club-throwing
- Swinging with a fearful image of what you want to avoid

Rate On a 1 to 5 Scale

There are some habits you might like to change that are not strictly yes or nos, but instead manifest in degrees. For these you can use a rating scale. First, establish your intention of a habit you'd like to increase and/or one you'd like to decrease. Rate these on a scale of 1 to 5 (representing the maximum and minimum amount the habit appears). For example, you may have a tendency to guide your tee shots rather than releasing through the swing freely, which you'd rather do. Rate each tee shot, assigning a 1 to shots that you guide the most and 5 to shots that you release the most freely. Gradually, you'll see more and more ratings of 4 or 5, meaning freer and freer swings.

Dorothy would make a beautiful, free practice swing and then make a dreadful trying-too-hard slash at the ball. She established her intention to swing at the ball the way she took her practice swing (more trusting and less trying). She then rated how closely her swing at the ball matched her practice swing on the trusting (5) versus trying (1) dimension. After only nine holes, she had moved from mostly 1s and 2s to many more 4s and 5s on the rating scale and was hitting better shots than she ever had.

untie the sandbags

Bret, a top amateur player for several years, had just turned professional and qualified to play on one of the big tours. He started the year playing well, and other more experienced golfers were offering him encouragement and seemingly helpful suggestions. He learned more and more details about swing technique, but when he came to me, he was playing very poorly and feeling miserable. "Doc, I know so much more about the golf swing, and I think my swing is technically better than it was six months ago, but it seems like I've forgotten how to score."

"Mental game obstacles are like sandbags tied to your body. How well would you swing if you had sandbags hanging from your wrists, hips, knees, elbows, and neck?" I explained. Bret said he already felt that way. I said, "My job is to help you identify the sandbags and untie each of the knots so the bags fall off. With each one that you untie, you'll be more and more free to make the swing you already know how to make.

"In golf they don't have judges rating the technical merit of the swing, as in diving or gymnastics or figure skating. They don't give style points. The problem is that you're playing 'golf-swing' instead of playing golf. You're so worried about how you're swinging that it's getting in the way of just playing. If you're thinking about how to swing, you're thinking, not swinging. Here's your assignment: Go out tomorrow, don't keep score, just have fun. Enjoy hitting a golf ball without worrying about how you're hitting it or where it's going to go. The only thing you need to do is to write the word 'Worries' on your scorecard and mark down each time you worry about your swing. Once you've marked it down, forget about it and go on to your next shot."

The next time we spoke, Bret was very happy. "For the first time in months I really enjoyed myself on the golf course. Even though I did have twelve 'Worries,' mostly I just played the way I used to: picking my target and sending the ball there. And I made a whole bunch of birdies!"

With each round he played, Bret had fewer worries about his swing, got better results, and enjoyed playing golf a whole lot more.

fire your evil caddie

Do you talk to yourself on the golf course? Out loud, silently, or a bit of both? Most of us engage in some form of self-talk. We don't usually pay much attention to the quality of what we're saying, but perhaps we should. The way people talk about something to themselves is a reflection of how they feel about it. If we say, "I don't have much of a chance on this shot," we're not likely to do well. On the other hand, if we say, "I can see what I need to do and how to do it," we are more likely to succeed.

What we say to ourselves has a powerful impact on our game. That's because we're not just talking—we're listening. What we hear about ourselves affects how we feel about ourselves, and how we feel about ourselves affects our performance. In my golf schools I introduce this topic using a role-playing exercise called Fire Your Evil Caddie. I ask for a volunteer from the participants and we pretend to be a golfer and caddie on the first tee about to start a round. As the caddie handing him his driver, I say, "Remember all the things you're supposed to do in your swing. Everybody's watching now, so try not to make a fool of yourself. You're making people wait—why don't you just get it over with? And try not to slice it into the woods like you usually do." After the volunteer pretends to swing, I say, "That was terrible! I knew you were going to slice it into the woods. Won't you ever learn how to play this game?"

At that point I turn to the participants and ask what they'd do with a caddie like that. They usually reply in unison: "Fire him!"

Then I ask, "Have you ever said any of those things to yourself during a round of golf?" A wave of recognition sweeps through the group, accompanied by groans of remorse. I explain, "Talking to yourself that way is like taking an evil caddie around with you for eighteen holes. Why don't you fire your evil caddie and be your own best friend?"

isn't where you have to play it from punishment enough?

We're so hard on ourselves. We tie our self-worth to the results of our actions, to how well we hit a golf shot or what score we make on a hole. When things go badly, we start to doubt our basic goodness as human beings. We start to say things like "What's wrong with me?"

We usually can't accept making a mistake, despite the fact that we know everybody makes them. Here's an exercise that illustrates this point. I ask everyone to imagine that a good friend has just hit a bad shot. Then I ask them to put their friend's name in the sentence: "That's okay, [friend's name], everybody makes mistakes." Imagining that we are each saying it to our friend in an actual situation, we all say the sentence together. We do it a few times to get the feeling. Then we discuss how the exercise felt. In general, people say they feel good about being able to give support and comfort to a friend.

Then part two of the exercise is introduced. I ask them to say the same sentence but now use their own name instead of their friend's. When they say the sentence, most of their voices are barely audible. I ask them to say it again. Many people have painful looks on their faces. Some laugh nervously to avoid the tension. Some say they feel their chests constrict or their throats tighten up.

Most of us find it much easier to say, "That's okay, everybody makes mistakes," to a friend than to ourselves. In general, people give themselves a really hard time, and have a really hard time giving themselves a break.

Like having an evil caddie, we sometimes beat ourselves up all the way around the course. If we're playing poorly, let's not add insult to injury. If we hit a bad shot, isn't where we have to play it from punishment enough?

accentuate the positive

The mental skills necessary to play your best golf need to be learned and "grooved" just as good swing techniques do. Proper mental habits need to be ingrained to supplant unhelpful ones. One such unhelpful habit is the tendency to focus on the negative, which needs to be replaced by accentuating the positive. A conversation with a touring professional provides a good illustration of this point.

After the first round of a tournament, I asked Andy how the day went. "I played okay, more or less. I had one hole where I chose the wrong club and made double-bogey." It sounded to me like he'd come in at 1 or 2 over par. Later that day I was looking at the scoreboard and was completely surprised when I saw his hole-by-hole score. In our conversation, he'd neglected to mention that he'd made an eagle and four birdies.

So often we emphasize the negative and disregard the positive. We're often our own worst critics, finding something wrong in almost every shot, even the good ones. We have some idea (probably one we've had most of our lives) that if we don't make a big deal about a mistake we've made, we'll never learn from it. So if a shot doesn't come off just the way we planned, we give ourselves a hard time.

It takes practice and patience to break habits like negative self-talk. The first step is awareness. Pay attention to what you say about each shot or about your round. You'll probably be surprised at how often you make a negative comment. Instead, find something good about every shot, about every round, to replace the habit of complaining or criticizing.

A further step is to let go of the errors and dwell on the successes. Take the time to appreciate a good shot as it flies to the target and settles down just where you planned. This will imprint a positive image in your mind and build your confidence. After a round, spend a few minutes reviewing the good decisions and the good shots you made.

There's a particular situation I'd like to address: average golfers who get upset because they hit a shot better than they expected, a drive so solid that it runs through the fairway into the rough or an approach shot so pure that it flies the green. They miss the joy of feeling that pure shot. Yes, you got a bad break, but only because you hit an especially good shot. Fixating on the result robs you of the experience, and you end up feeling bad instead of good. On top of that, a lingering negative attitude about the shot will interfere with your ability to play your next shot. Finally, feeling bad about the result of a good shot sends a negative message to your body about hitting shots like that. With that message, you'll certainly do your best to avoid hitting one that well in the future. Wouldn't it be better to feel good about the *process* (regardless of the result), and send a message to your body that you'd like more where that came from? Focus on the feeling of hitting a great shot—if you find yourself facing this situation frequently, it means you're improving.

uplifted body, uplifted mind

There is a very clear correspondence between our state of mind and how our body manifests. When our mind has anxiety or fear, our body feels tight and agitated. When we are discouraged or depressed, our body feels heavy and sluggish. When we are confident and at ease, our body feels energetic and responsive.

Our mental state affects our posture, how our body looks as we stand or walk. As we watch golfers walking up the eighteenth fairway, it's not hard to tell which ones are playing well

and which ones are playing poorly. The golfers who are playing poorly seem to be dragging along, shoulders hunched,
head down, looking at the ground, maybe even muttering to
themselves. The golfers who are playing well have a bounce in
their step. They walk tall, shoulders back, head up, looking
straight ahead, maybe even whistling to themselves.

Recognizing the effect our mind has on our body can help
us understand the importance of maintaining a positive, supportive attitude toward ourselves. If we become self-critical after a poor shot, telling ourselves how bad we are, our body
will feel more tense, have less energy, and be less responsive.
That will make for more bad shots, more self-criticism, and
establish a cycle of negativity that guarantees a miserable
round of golf.

The next time you hit a poor shot, remember that even
great players hit poor shots on occasion, and even have days
with lots of poor shots. Then focus on the next shot you have
to play, drawing on a past experience when you hit that same
type of shot very well. This will send a more confident message to your body, and your body will be more likely to produce the shot you're looking for.

Not only does our mind affect our body, but our body also
sends messages to our mind. If we walk slumped over, looking
at the ground, it confirms to our mind that things are going
badly. Then we feel more discouraged and our body feels less
energetic, starting a negative chain reaction that gets worse
and worse.

Instead, as you walk between shots, whether good or bad,

maintain an upright posture, shoulders back, taking full breaths. Humming or whistling softly can make you feel more relaxed and positive. Look up and out to the horizon, or even higher (at the treetops or clouds). Directing your eyes up and out creates a feeling of spaciousness and larger perspective that makes it easier to let go of the past and focus on the next shot.

No matter how you've been playing, maintaining a confident posture will make you feel more positive. And that will give you the best state of mind for the next shot you face.

you can't stop the waves, but you can learn to surf

My teacher, Ösel Tendzin, had a favorite response when his meditation students would ask how to control their thoughts and emotions. He'd say, "You can't stop the waves, but you can learn to surf. One person will struggle with the waves and be battered about. Another person will learn to ride them. Same waves, very different experiences."

We experience waves of emotions through the course of a tournament, a round of golf, or even a single golf hole. If we can ride the ups and downs with poise, humor, and humility, it makes the game more enjoyable for ourselves and our playing companions. To do so depends on perspective.

When you're in contention in a match or tournament, you're likely to feel waves of nervousness. Taking them as a bad sign will undermine your confidence. If you try to suppress them, you make them more distracting. They become a drain on your energy. That's like trying to stop the waves.

Instead, learn to surf on the waves of nervousness. Why are you feeling that way? Because you're in contention. Even the greatest golfers have felt nervous in big tournaments. But they use the energy, like surfers use the energy of the waves. They thrive on the feeling, because it means they are where they want to be—playing well with a chance to win. If you weren't playing well, what would you have to be nervous about? Taking nervousness as a sign that things are going well, instead of a harbinger of disaster, makes all the difference in the world.

why are you still carrying her?

Once there were two monks walking along a path through the woods. When they came to a stream, they encountered a young woman dressed in fine silks, unable to get across without ruining her clothes. One of the monks offered to carry her on his back. She climbed on, they all crossed the stream, and on the other side he set her down. She thanked him, and the two monks continued on their way.

The monastery to which these monks belonged had a rule prohibiting them from touching women. The other monk was horrified that his brother in the order had broken this rule, and was agonizing about it as they walked. He thought, "How could he violate his vows like this? Will he confess? Should I tell the abbot? Will they throw him out? Will I get in trouble, too? Why did he put me in this situation?" And he got more and more upset.

Finally, after they'd gone about a mile, he stopped abruptly and shouted, "How could you do that?"

"Do what?" asked the first monk.

"How could you touch that woman?"

"Oh, her? I set her down when we got across the stream. Why, my brother, are you still carrying her on your back?"

This story points to the fact that when something upsetting happens, we have a tendency to ruminate about it. We can stew about things for a long, long time. Being preoccupied with the past makes it impossible to do our best in the present. It's all too common for a player to make a mistake on the first hole and then be very distracted for several holes afterward, still agonizing over the mistake. Needless to say, the quality of play on those holes is far less than stellar.

It's critical to let go of any mishap as soon as possible. When a hole is done, you put the score on the card, and that's it. There's nothing more you can do about it. Let it go and focus on what's next. If thoughts about the previous hole keep coming up, do your best to let them go by as in "Dive Under the Waves."

If this is a regular occurrence, you can use the technique of intention plus nonjudgmental awareness presented earlier in "Pebbles in the Bowl." Without judging or criticizing yourself, make a mark each time you have a thought about a previous mistake. Such thoughts will arise less and less, and you will be able to focus on the only shot that matters: the one you're playing now.

these things come and go

A long time ago, there was a queen who was very thoughtful. She truly wished the best for all her people and always sought to improve herself so she could be a wiser and better ruler. In contemplating her own experience, she took note of her reactions when things went particularly well or poorly.

When things were going especially well, she sometimes got a swelled head, feeling proud and arrogant. At times she became complacent, feeling that things would just continue to go well without any effort. Other times she charged ahead, assuming her good fortune would hold, dangerously overextending the resources of the kingdom.

When things were going especially poorly, she had a tendency to complain, fretting about what to do and getting depressed about her misfortune. Her hopelessness would leave her *with no interest in doing anything. She felt that things would continue to go badly, so what was the use?*

Disturbed by these tendencies in herself, she sought the counsel of her advisers. This was her request:

"I seek instructions that will help me temper my pride, complacency, and recklessness when things go well, and will also uplift me from my depression, complaining, and inaction when things go poorly."

Her advisers gave her elaborate plans for each of a wide variety of situations. But these were too complicated. "How can I possibly remember to do all these things in all these situations?"

Then the old chambermaid spoke up, respectfully but with confidence. "Your Majesty, I have five words that will provide you with what you need no matter what the situation, whether extremely good or extremely bad, that will temper your pride and lighten your burden. You only have to remember:

"These things come and go."

It's undeniably true that all of our experiences are temporary. Impermanence, the inevitability of change, is one of the most basic teachings of Buddhism. The importance of this for the human condition is not the physical fact of impermanence, but our reaction to it. If we can't accept the fact that everything changes, then change will be a source of suffering. If we overreact to a bad shot, we suffer. Wouldn't it make more sense to accept the percentage of missed shots that fits our handicap?

We can think outside the box about impermanence as well. If the present situation never changed, we'd all be statues. Impermanence is *necessary* for one moment to change into the next. If we don't "die" to our old way of playing golf, a new way of playing golf can never come into existence.

Since "pride goeth before a fall," golf is a wonderful messenger of impermanence about our ability to master the game. In one round we proclaim to ourselves, "Now I've got it!" and when we come back the next day, it's nowhere to be found.

This version of the Serenity Prayer is very helpful in dealing with the ups and downs of golf:

> May I have the courage to accomplish what I can,
> May I have the patience to accept what I can't accomplish,
> And may I have the wisdom to know the difference between the two.

overcoming self-sabotage

Everyone has comfort levels. They are the levels of performance or spheres of activity that are familiar to us. And we're comfortable with what is familiar. We're comfortable playing in the B-flight, we're comfortable chasing the leader from behind, we're comfortable just making the cut. We're comfortable playing our usual game.

Sabotage is the undermining (through underhanded interference) of a project or mission. Self-sabotage doesn't make sense—why would we undermine our own work to reach an important goal (like breaking 80)? Yet the decisions we make and the way we perform make it look like that's exactly what we're doing. There's a twist. What looks like self-sabotage is actually self-protection.

What are we protecting ourselves from? Stress, anxiety, discomfort. We're protecting ourselves from leaving our comfort levels.

One day we're playing better than we ever have. Someone points out how well we're doing, we immediately feel like we're playing "over our head," and we make two double-bogeys in a row. Because it was unfamiliar territory, we became more careful. We tried extra hard because we didn't think our regular game was good enough to keep playing at that level. Being more careful and trying extra hard interfere with playing good golf. In other words, we were outside our comfort level and found a way to get back to it in a hurry.

Trying to break 80 is something we're familiar with, but shooting in the 70s isn't. We're about to break 80 for the first time, needing only a 5 on the last hole. We hit our drive off the map, take 2 to get near the green, chili-dip a chip, and 3-putt for a 7. That way we get to keep on trying, an activity that's frustrating but familiar. And it's stressful just to think that our new job will be to try to break 75.

In the club championship, we're poised to win the B-flight when we hit our drive on the last hole out-of-bounds and lose by a stroke. We know the guys in the B-flight, and get to keep being one of the best B-golfers. That's a lot more comfortable than being the low man on the totem pole with the hot-shots in the A-flight.

Comfort levels involve expectations, some real and some imagined. If you shoot a particularly low score, you might think that everyone will expect you to play to that level from now on. Imagining the future expectations of golf partners and club members can create sufficient anxiety for a golfer to come apart at the seams in the last few holes. One of my students was an older golfer who said he was afraid that if he shot any low scores, his partners would make him play from the blue tees. He expected to play poorly from the blue tees and look bad, so he continued to play just badly enough from the white tees to stay there. During our playing lesson, we played from the blue tees. At first he struggled but soon found that it wasn't as hard as he'd imagined. On the back nine he shot about the same score as he usually did from the white tees. His comfort level had expanded, and the next round he shot his career best from the white tees. He plays from the blue tees now.

Self-sabotage often appears in high-pressure situations. We'd like to turn in our best performance; however, avoiding or escaping anxiety commands a higher priority. This isn't a conscious decision. It is our instinct to protect ourselves from the embarrassment, disappointment, and self-recrimination that we anticipate if we don't measure up.

One way we protect ourselves from failure is by not trying.

Linking our self-worth to how well we play golf is the problem. If our best game isn't good enough, our self-esteem will take a beating. To avoid that, when the going gets tough, we quit, don't give it our all, get careless. The subconscious logic is: If I didn't really try, I didn't really fail. We might feel bad about losing a match, but it's far less painful than feeling bad about ourselves.

Another way we sabotage ourselves in a stressful situation is trying a much harder shot than necessary, such as trying to carry a hazard that would require the best shot we ever hit. If we fail, we can blame the fact that it was a next-to-impossible shot. We can rationalize that we didn't really fail; we just made a bad decision.

What can we do to prevent self-sabotage? The first step is to recognize it. Use the body scan to observe your body, and awareness practice to observe your thoughts. First, notice how much tension you're feeling, and see if the level of anxiety is disproportionate to the difficulty of the shot you face. You may have added extra meaning to the situation that raises the stakes and invites self-sabotage.

Next, notice your impulses. Do you feel the urge to get the shot over with? Do you feel like it's all too much and you don't care what happens? Does the shot you've chosen suggest delusions of grandeur? These are all indicators that there's self-sabotage afoot.

When you recognize the symptoms, you can apply remedies. Describe the circumstances to yourself in a different way. Think of a five-foot putt as just what it is—a ball, five feet of grass, and a hole—rather than a five-foot putt *for your second birdie in a row.* Focus on your routine, on the process rather than the results. Use your breathing to settle yourself and connect with your center of gravity. When you find yourself thinking about upcoming holes or what you'll say if you win the tournament, bring yourself back to the present, dive under the wave of thoughts, and refocus on the shot at hand.

There will be times when self-sabotage wins out. Recognize it, reflect on it (without judging yourself), and learn from it. See how your attachment to a comfort level interfered with accomplishing your intentions. Be aware of your feelings in similar situations. As they become more familiar, you'll be better able to manage them. In that way you can overcome self-sabotage and take your game to the next level.

patience pays

Many years ago in Japan, a student came to a master of kendo* and said, "If I become your devoted student, how long will it take for me to master the sword?"

The master replied, "Perhaps ten years."

"That's a long time," said the student. "If I try really hard, how long would it take me?"

---

*The art of Zen swordsmanship; literally "the way of the sword."

The master replied, "Oh, maybe twenty years."

The student was shocked. "First you said ten, now you say twenty years. What if I try as hard as I can?"

"Well," said the master, "in that case it will take thirty years. Someone as impatient for results as you will probably take a long time to learn anything."

In golf we often fall victim to impatience. Golfers have a tendency to look for the secret, the magic tip, that will make the swing work perfectly, instantly, and forever. They want it all and they want it now. But it doesn't work that way. Like anything in life, if you haven't addressed the fundamentals, quick fixes don't hold up. There's no substitute for repeating good habits with awareness until the movements become natural.

Practice with a purpose, practice with a plan, practice with patience. If you're working on something, have the patience to feel confidence in it before you take it out on the course. Train it until you trust it, and trust it before you try it.

If you play while you're working on something, it's very important to stick with it *without expectation of getting immediate results*. It takes commitment. It takes patience. Impatience for results is the reason many amateurs don't benefit from swing instruction lessons.

When a lesson involves making a swing change, most golfers experience a period of poor performance. They find themselves "between swings": very self-conscious about how they are swinging the club and very inconsistent in their ball striking. Before any improvement starts to appear, they have to weather a time of playing far worse than they are used to. Unfortunately, golfers often give up too soon and go back to their old way of swinging. At that point they get an immediate improvement in performance (from "worse than ever" back to "the usual") and decide that their old swing was better for them and that the lesson didn't work.

They may feel better about their game, but they ended up right back where they started. If they had kept practicing and accepted the bad results as a temporary phenomenon, after some time their performance would have surpassed their original level and they would have experienced real improvement.

Both Nick Faldo and Tiger Woods reworked their swings at points in their careers when they were already winning. They felt they had the potential to play better and win even more often, especially in major tournaments. They were willing to accept a period of lesser results for the future reward of reaching new levels when their new swing became a natural motion. They got their rewards.

take your medicine

Impatience compounds mistakes. Making a poor shot, we should accept the situation and play the smartest shot from there. Instead, we try to make it all up with the next shot. If we miss a few putts, we begin pressing to get our approach shots closer to the pin, often taking unwarranted risks and suffering the consequences.

Stephen had been playing golf for just three years, but had taken lessons regularly. Still, he had never broken 100. His pro suggested a lesson with me. He hit a few balls and seemed to have a pretty reasonable swing. He said that his short game wasn't great, but he two-putted most of the time. So what caused him to take so many strokes? Impatience.

Being a relative beginner, he would mis-hit quite a few tee shots each round. Every time that happened, he'd try to get it all back in one mighty blow—a disastrous tactic, of course. This is a common mistake among high handicappers. It leads to the succession of topped shots and screaming slices that come from swinging with all one's might, as well as the injudicious decisions to play shots that most pros wouldn't even attempt.

After discussing this approach and its futility, we agreed that he would try to accept the consequence of each mis-hit and not compound the error by trying to get more on the next shot than could be reasonably expected. I introduced two fundamental principles of course management: Play a shot you're comfortable playing, and give yourself the easiest next shot. Here's an example of the game plan we devised:

A topped tee shot that goes 125 yards on a 400-yard hole leaves 275 yards. Usually, Stephen would try to get as close to the green as he could with a three-wood and end up in trouble. But now he was to "take his medicine" and accept the consequence of the poor tee shot. This meant playing the hole as if it were a par-5. For his second shot, he was to use a club that would put him in comfortable range for his pitching wedge or nine-iron. He hit his nine-iron about 120 yards, so all he needed was a 155-yard shot to the middle of the fairway, a relatively easy, low-pressure shot. This way he would be almost assured of a 5 on the hole, have a chance to make a putt for a 4, and have removed the possibility of a 7 or higher.

His next time out, Stephen began by taking a 9 on the first hole. This served as a wake-up call; he remembered his game plan and stuck to it for the rest of the round. With this strategy he shot 95, breaking 100 for the first time by a large margin.

how to enjoy
a bad round of golf

Often a golfer will have a bad start to a round and get completely depressed, assuming that the day will go that way. His discouragement creates a self-fulfilling prophecy. But since each hole is physically independent of the others, isn't it possible that the rest of the round will be the best he ever played? What a different round he might have had if he took that perspective.

Sometimes we struggle and struggle until late in the round

when we say, "Oh, I give up. I'm just going to get up there and hit it." And to our surprise the shot comes off well. That's because we didn't really give up. We let go. Letting go can transform our round. When we let go of trying, there's no interference to making a free, smooth swing.

Your perspective on score affects how you feel about your round. Realize that your handicap corresponds roughly to the average of the *best* ten of your last twenty rounds. If you feel it's a bad round when you don't play to your handicap or better, you'll be frustrated with about three-fourths of your rounds. If you aren't happy unless your score is near your career best, you'll be dissatisfied most all the time. Your day will be far more enjoyable if you don't obsess over how you stand in relation to par (gross or net) as you play each hole.

You can't know for certain if it's a bad round until the round's over. What if you were playing worse than usual but on number seventeen you got a hole-in-one? That wouldn't be such a bad round. Let go of the poor result you had on the last hole and you have a lot better chance of enjoying the hole you're playing now. When we spend less time worrying about the score, there's more space in our minds for fun.

Make a commitment to finding a way to enjoy yourself regardless of how you're scoring. Stay true to that commitment and there won't be any such thing as a bad round. If you remember to appreciate the scenery and the company of your fellow golfers, you can enjoy a round even if your score is higher than usual. When you consider some of the alternatives, you can recognize how fortunate you are just to be out on a golf course, regardless of your score. Turn your attention from your internal monologue to the vividness of your senses. Connect with the environment and notice what you see, hear, feel, and smell. When you're not struggling, you might be surprised to find that the swing you thought was lost has miraculously reappeared.

Another helpful approach is to shift your focus from performance to learning. Use every round, good score or not, as a learning experience. Make your goal to learn as much as possible about the game and about yourself. It could be a great day if, during a so-called bad round, you learned something that made every future round more enjoyable.

One cause of a bad round is thinking about your final score before you tee off. Expectations about score interfere with playing your best. A friend of mine started the second day of a tournament with the thought "If I play well, I might win." When he expressed disappointment with his round, I asked if his words "play well" had actually meant "score well." They had, and his own expectations had put pressure on him and introduced tension into his swing. This led to poor shots, more pressure, more tension, and a high score. He had set himself up for a bad round.

If he had truly meant "play well," he would have focused on the process, staying present and trusting his routine and his swing. There's no guarantee, but intending to "play well" in this way would have given him the best chance of making good swings, the best chance of a low score, and the best chance of winning. His statement was absolutely true: If he played well, he might win. But even if he didn't win, by staying with his process his shots would have been far more satisfying. Then no matter what the score, it wouldn't have been a bad round.

who knows what's good and what's bad?

*L*ong ago, there was an old farmer living on the outskirts of a little village. He was quite poor, possessing only a small piece of land, a small house in which he lived with his only son, and one horse.

One day, the horse broke out of the corral and ran away. The neighbors came over to console the farmer. They said, "Oh, this is so terrible! You were poor before, but now you're destitute. What bad luck! This is the worst thing that could have happened."

The old farmer shrugged his shoulders and gently said, "Who knows what's good and what's bad?"

The farmer fixed the fence and left the gate open. The next day, his horse came back and went right into the corral, followed by a whole herd of wild horses. The neighbors came over to congratulate him. They said, "Oh, this is so wonderful! You were the poorest man in the village and now you're the richest. What good fortune! This is the best thing that could have happened."

The old farmer shrugged his shoulders and again said, "Who knows what's good and what's bad."

The next day, his son was working to tame the new horses. One of them bucked and he fell off, breaking his leg. The neighbors came over and said, "Oh, this is so terrible! Now your son is hurt, the horses can't be tamed, and you have no one to help you harvest your crop. What bad luck! This is the worst thing that could have happened!"

The old farmer shrugged his shoulders and once more said, "Who knows what's good and what's bad?"

And the next day, the king's army came through the countryside, taking all the able-bodied young men off to battle, where they were almost sure to die. But because the old farmer's son's leg was hurt, he wasn't taken along. So who knows what's good and what's bad?

All too often when something happens that seems especially good or bad, we project into the past and the future. We regret and relive a bad event, imagining that if it had gone the other way, everything would have worked out so much better. But that's pure fantasy. There's no way to know how things *would* have worked out. We might think, "Life would be so much better if only I'd made that putt and won the tournament." But winning a tournament doesn't guarantee that we'll live happily ever after. There are many stories of Rookies of the Year who weren't ready for what success brought to their lives, lost track of their game, and never returned to that level.

Kathy Whitworth, one of the greatest golfers of all time, said she felt very fortunate that it took her several years to win. She felt that learning how to accept losing prepared her to be a better winner.

We might make what we think is a great deal and then find out that the market for that product has disappeared. We might miss our airplane flight and then meet someone at the airport who turns out to be a fantastic business contact. Like golf, life is unpredictable.

When Jack Nicklaus won his last Masters Championship in 1986, his short putt on the twelfth hole hit a spike mark and veered off-line, giving him a bogey. That seemingly bad occurrence fired him up, and he went on to shoot 30 on the back nine for a 65 and his record sixth Green Jacket. So who knows what's good and what's bad?

PART 3

A Game of Honor

In the Shambhala tradition, discipline is connected with how to become thoroughly gentle and genuine. It shows you how to make the journey, and guides you in the way of the warrior. It is unwavering and all-pervasive. To be a warrior is to learn to be genuine in every moment of your life. The warrior never gives up.

—Venerable Chögyam Trungpa,
*Shambhala: The Sacred Path
of the Warrior*

chi chi's prayer

I never prayed that I would make a putt. I prayed that
I would react well if I missed.

—Chi Chi Rodriguez,
Senior PGA Tour veteran

A teaching professional who was an old friend of mine had just moved to a new town and started work at the local golf course. I was visiting, and we went to another nearby course for a round of golf. There were a number of people around the first tee as we were about to start. He said to me, "I'm pretty nervous."

I said, "What have you got to be nervous about? You're a better golfer than anyone for a hundred miles."

He said, "But what will people think of me if I hit a bad shot? They won't want to take lessons from me. So my livelihood is on the line for this shot. That's why I'm nervous."

I said, "I don't think that's quite accurate. Everybody knows that even good players hit poor shots on occasion. They won't be concerned if you miss. They'll be concerned about how you *handle* it if you miss. They know a PGA pro has the information; they want a pro who knows how to conduct himself."

Using the post-shot routine presented earlier is the ideal way to handle both good and bad results. If you hit a poor shot, you have the choice of keeping your cool rather than beating yourself up with a string of epithets.

Keeping your cool doesn't mean stifling your emotions. That can make them build up under the surface until you blow your top. It's natural to feel some frustration after a shot has gone awry. The key is to feel it and then quickly *get over it* so you can get on with the business of playing the next shot.

You can experience your emotions without indulging in cursing, moaning, and making a scene. Reacting that way is a habit you can change by applying intention and nonjudgmental awareness.

On your scorecard write a phrase that describes your habit: club tossing, temper tantrum, hissy fit, etc. Make a mark each time you engage in the habit, without judging yourself. If you have a strong intention to change, the habit will recur less and less. And you and your playing companions will enjoy the game more and more.

shambhala golf

Confidence is a change in attitude that makes the seemingly unworkable workable. This doesn't mean that all of a sudden everything is going to go our way. But it does mean that we can appreciate life even when things don't go our way. We have the resources to live in the challenge. That is the expression of the courage of a Shambhala warrior.

—Venerable Chögyam Trungpa, *Shambhala: The Sacred Path of the Warrior*

Like the legend of King Arthur and Camelot, Shambhala is a legendary kingdom that is a model of enlightened society. The people there live and relate with each other in an open and compassionate way, embodying bravery, genuineness, confidence, and dignity. In Camelot these qualities were realized in "knighthood"; in the Shambhala tradition they manifest as "warriorship." Shambhala warriorship is not about conquering others and wreaking destruction. It is about having the bravery to overcome aggression, to manifest fearless gentleness.

The fundamental training of a Shambhala warrior is based on the Buddhist practices of mindfulness and awareness. The warrior's "basic training" is formal sitting meditation. The complement to sitting practice is mindfulness and awareness in action. As in Zen, these are practiced as Shambhala disciplines in a variety of forms such as flower arranging, calligraphy, tea ceremony, and martial arts including kendo (swordsmanship) and kyudo (archery).

Ösel Tendzin, my meditation teacher who was also an avid golfer, encouraged his students to relate to the game of golf in a similar way: as a venue for practicing mindfulness and awareness, as well as developing insight and compassion. He taught four principles for playing Shambhala golf, ways of transforming our outlook and experience: how we play and how we feel while we're playing. They became the basis of how I aspired to play the game, to relate with others on the course, and to coach the mental game of golf.

The Four Principles

Virtue

Virtue is the expression of basic goodness in action. Basic goodness is the fundamental worthiness of every individual. In playing golf, what matters most is experience without the reference point of results. Ultimately, the outcome of the game is neither important nor unimportant. The real point is that it is good to be mutually engaged in our world, joining body, mind, and heart in the vividness of the moment. This is the ground for discovering unconditional confidence.

Discipline

Discipline means proper conduct. Because of virtue, we understand proper conduct as that which overcomes pettiness. In golf we make a relationship to the form of the game and our interactions with others. When frustration arises, it becomes the working basis for developing discipline. By applying generosity, ethics, patience, exertion, equanimity, and insight, we can transcend pettiness and irritation. Therefore, discipline is the antidote to the negativity that can arise while playing the game of golf, and the means to cultivate a confident and uplifted attitude.

Humor

Humor is the absence of self-importance. Humor brings a quality of lightness, an atmosphere of enjoyment. It does not refer to frivolous comments at someone else's expense or the ability to tell a joke. Rather, it is a simple and genuine delight in participating in the game of golf. With humor we can avoid the self-defeating habits of taking ourselves too seriously or being too heavily focused on results. With humor we can relax and trust ourselves and be able to help others do the same.

Friendship

Playing the game of golf is a wonderful way of engaging in our world and appreciating our life. Through virtue, discipline, and humor, the simplicity of the game becomes the stepping-stone for believing in ourselves and opening our heart to others. An open heart is the basis of true friendship: accepting all the qualities we experience in our fellow human beings and ourselves. This is the foundation for expanding a vision of openness and compassion throughout the world.

a warrior's dignity

A Zen student went for an interview with his master. The student said, "I know this may require a very lengthy and complex answer, but I request guidelines for conducting myself wherever I am, so that my attitude and behavior are always excellent."

The master said, "Actually, the answer is quite brief and simple: In every situation, conduct yourself as if your five-year-old child were watching you."

Golf is a perfect venue for the expression of a Shambhala warrior's dignity. It is probably the only sport that begins its set of rules with a chapter on etiquette. First you learn how to conduct yourself on the course, *then* you learn the rules of the game. In no other major sport do professionals call penalties on themselves when they violate the rules, even unknowingly.

Players who depend on their winnings for their livelihood nevertheless offer assistance and advice to other players who are competing against them. Even during competition, players will help each other look for a lost ball. At the Masters Tournament one year, with both players in contention on the back nine on Sunday, Lee Janzen was actively searching through the bushes behind one of the greens looking for Greg Norman's ball.

Mutual respect and honor are the deepest expressions of friendship. When we have made friends with ourselves, we see the extent to which others have not, and compassion arises in our heart. Feeling unconditional confidence, we're not afraid to extend ourselves to others.

Ray Floyd said something that I feel truly expresses a Shambhala warrior's dignity. He was asked how he'd like to be remembered. In other sports (or business or politics for that matter), top performers might say that they want to be remembered as the greatest of this, the best of that, holding the record for this, that, and the other. But Ray Floyd, a record holder and great champion himself, said, "When a father takes his son out for his first game of golf, and he says, 'Son, when you're on the golf course, I want you to always conduct yourself like a gentleman—I want you to conduct yourself like Ray Floyd,' that's how I'd like to be remembered."

gentle, inquisitive, fearless

Playing the game of golf can inspire us to embody gentleness, inquisitiveness, and fearlessness. Gentleness means being kind to ourselves and considerate of others. We can take delight in conducting ourselves as gentle men and gentle women in golf and in life.

Inquisitiveness happens in the space of big mind, expansive and open to the vividness of the moment. Regarding results as more "interesting" than frustrating, insight dawns unimpeded. Intention and nonjudgmental awareness provide the atmosphere for continuous learning and growth.

Fearlessness means being more curious than afraid, trusting in our basic goodness and manifesting unconditional confidence in every situation we encounter.

These are the most fundamental qualities of Shambhala warriorship. Through golf and every other activity, the ultimate goal of a Shambhala warrior is to foster an enlightened society, an environment in which individuals manifest peace, openness, and compassion in relating to themselves and others.

Zen Golf presents methods by which you can transform your approach to the game of golf and the game of life. It is my hope that this book has helped you to awaken the sunshine of awareness and reveal the infinite possibilities before you. May it arouse your basic goodness to inspire unconditional confidence in yourself and those you encounter, on the golf course and everywhere you go.

index of exercises

(Page number indicates beginning of exercise within a chapter.)

references and recommended reading

Beck, Charlotte Joko. *Everyday Zen.* New York: HarperCollins, 1989.

Benson, Herbert. *The Relaxation Response.* New York: William Morrow, 1975.

Chödrön, Pema. *Start Where You Are: A Guide to Compassionate Living.* Boston: Shambhala, 1994.

Gallwey, W. Timothy. *The Inner Game of Golf.* New York: Random House, 1981.

Hahn, Thich Nhat. *The Miracle of Mindfulness.* Boston: Beacon Press, 1975.

———. *Peace Is Every Step.* New York: Bantam, 1991.

Haultain, Arnold. *The Mystery of Golf.* Boston: Houghton Mifflin, 2000. (Reprint of the 1908 original.)

Herrigel, Eugen. *Zen in the Art of Archery.* Pantheon Books, 1953.

Jones, Bobby. *Golf Is My Game.* London: Chatto and Windus, 1962.

Kabat-Zinn, Jon. *Wherever You Go, There You Are.* New York: Hyperion, 1994.

McLeod, Ken. *Wake Up to Your Life.* New York: HarperCollins, 2001.

Moffitt, Phillip. *Dancing with Life.* New York: Rodale, 2008.

Murphy, Michael. *Golf in the Kingdom.* New York: Viking Press, 1972.

Nicklaus, Jack. *Golf My Way.* New York: Simon and Schuster, 1974.

———. *Jack Nicklaus' Playing Lessons.* Trumbull, Conn.: Golf Digest Books, 1981.

Parent, Joseph. *Golf: The Art of the Mental Game.* New York: Universe, 2009.

Parent, Joseph. *Zen Putting: Mastering the Mental Game on the Greens.* New York: Gotham, 2007.

Penick, Harvey. *The Wisdom of Harvey Penick.* Collected writings. New York: Simon and Schuster, 1997.

Reps, Paul, and Nyogen Senzaki. *Zen Flesh, Zen Bones.* Boston: Tuttle Publishing, 1957.

Shoemaker, Fred. *Extraordinary Golf: The Art of the Possible.* New York: G. P. Putnam's Sons, 1996.

Simpson, W. G. *The Art of Golf.* Far Hills, N.J.: United States Golf Association, 1982. (Reprint of the 1887 original.)

Suzuki, Shunryu. *Zen Mind, Beginner's Mind.* New York: Weatherhill, 1970.

Tendzin, Ösel. *Buddha in the Palm of Your Hand.* Boston: Shambhala, 1982.

Trungpa, Chögyam. *Shambhala: The Sacred Path of the Warrior.* Boston: Shambhala, 1984.

———. *Great Eastern Sun.* Boston: Shambhala, 1999.

Vold, Mona. *Different Strokes: The Lives and Teachings of the Game's Wisest Women.* New York: Simon and Schuster, 1999.

Woods, Tiger. *How I Play Golf.* New York: Warner Books, 2001.

At the Top of Your Game™:
The Zen of Golf and Business

with Dr. Joseph Parent

Keynote Speaking, Executive Coaching,
Corporate Events,
Group and Individual Golf Lessons

Dr. Parent teaches at the spectacular Ojai Valley Inn
and Spa, a world-renowned golf resort in sunny
Southern California.

To learn more, please visit his website:

www.ZENGOLF.com
E-mail: **info@ZenGolf.com**
Telephone: (805) 640–1046